AF541560

FROM DEPENDENCE TO SELF-RELIANCE

Also by the author

The India Story: An Epic Journey of Democracy and Development

India Then & Now: An Insider's Account

India Ahead: 2025 and Beyond

Politics Trumps Economics: The Interface of Economics and Politics in Contemporary India (co-edited)

FROM DEPENDENCE TO SELF-RELIANCE

MAPPING INDIA'S RISE AS A GLOBAL SUPERPOWER

BIMAL JALAN

RUPA

First published by
Rupa Publications India Pvt. Ltd 2022
7/16, Ansari Road, Daryaganj
New Delhi 110002

Sales Centres:

Allahabad Bengaluru Chennai
Hyderabad Jaipur Kathmandu
Kolkata Mumbai

ISBN: 978-93-5520-378-6

First impression 2022

10 9 8 7 6 5 4 3 2 1

Printed in India

CONTENTS

PREFACE

From Dependence to Self-Reliance continues the strand of thought of my three earlier books—*India After Liberalisation: An Overview* (2021), *India Reckoning: Rewards and Discontents of Democracy* (2021) and *India Then & Now: An Insider's Account* (2020).While deciding on the content and structure of this book, I was principally guided by two considerations. First, it should be of interest to the general readers, in addition to policymakers and professional experts. Second, to make this volume relevant to the ongoing debate about India's approach to future economic growth, as well as governance and political issues in the twenty-first century.

Presently, the political profile of the government, with a single-party majority in Parliament, has changed dramatically. The government, elected with a full majority, is now in a position to launch political reforms on its own without relying on the discretionary powers of members belonging to other parties. This book highlights some important priorities that the government can implement at present, as well as in the future in light of past experience. The primary focus should be on promoting India's national interests, irrespective of any party's political agenda announced during elections (either on the Right or Left or a mix of both).

When it comes to the economy of the nation, it can be easily said that there are very few developing countries that are as well placed as India to take advantage of the phenomenal changes that have occurred in production technologies, international trade and deployment of skilled manpower. In view of these advantages, India is in a position to accelerate the growth rate of the economy to 7–8 per cent per annum over the next 25 years. The higher the growth of the economy, the greater is the capacity of the government to finance expenditure for essential social services. The combination of higher government expenditure on the provision of social services will provide higher growth in employment opportunities which will have a decisive impact in reducing poverty levels over time.

The book would not have been completed without mentioning the name of Satish Choudhary, for his meticulous work in preparing the manuscript for publication, and K.D. Sharma, for his organizational and other help. I am grateful to Yamini Chowdhury, senior commissioning editor, and her colleagues at Rupa Publications for their advice, guidance and painstaking efforts to edit and improve the contents of the book. I would also like to appreciate C. Sandhya for her excellent work in developing the manuscript. I also appreciate the work done by Manali Das in editing the book at relatively short notice. Without their help and support, this book could not have been written.

INTRODUCTION

From Dependence to Self-Reliance includes 10 chapters which are divided into three separate sections: Economy, Governance and Politics.

The first chapter is on the 'Current Situation and Future Prospects'. There is no doubt that in the twenty-first century, India's economy is on a new growth path. Part of the reasons for the resurgence of confidence in India's future is the implementation of economic reforms initiated in 1991, and the emergence of a majority-party government in 2014. With a single-party government in power, it is feasible to accelerate growth and reduce poverty as well as promote cooperative federalism between the Centre and the states. However, as it happens, on any global indicator of economic well-being—be it adult literacy, infant mortality, life expectancy or gender bias—India's actual performance remains among the bottom one-third among developing countries. A lot remains to be done before India is able to exploit the new opportunities to realize its full potential in the future. This chapter highlights the fact that the patterns of trade and investment have recently changed in India's favour. As such, if there is a strong political will to move ahead decisively to overcome the shortcomings in the policies and administrative practices of the past, India can become one of the leading economies in the world.

The next chapter on 'Science and Development' addresses some of the issues relating to science and technology. In addition, it also throws light on the relative roles of the state and the market in ensuring the impact of scientific knowledge in the culmination of technological know-how in a developing economy. India is perhaps the first country in the world to create a ministry of Scientific Research and Natural Resources as early as 1951 for organizing and directing scientific research aimed at national development. Since then, India has come a long way in its quest for scientific pursuit, both in the material and intellectual spheres. India now has the talent, the skills and the resources to be at the forefront of the technological revolution that is taking place in the new growth sectors of the global economy.

The third chapter is on 'Information Technology and Banking'. There is no doubt that these two sectors are vital for India's growth and broad-based development. There is a tremendous mutuality of interest in these two sectors. In the banking sector, information technology (IT) can reduce costs, increase volumes and facilitate customized financial products. Similarly, IT requires banking and financial services to facilitate its growth. Thus, financial services need IT, and IT needs financial services to make the maximum impact. At the same time, the fast growth of IT, compared with the relatively slower growth in banking services, has posed certain challenges. There are new opportunities for savers and investors to deal directly with each other rather than through the banking system unless banks can provide some value addition in terms of return and safety of funds or investment advice. This poses a challenge, particularly for public-sector banks.

The last chapter in Section 1 ('India's Stand in the Twenty-First Century') discusses the shift in the position that India holds in the twenty-first century and its implications on the nation's potential for growth. The chapter also discusses how a favourable shift in India's comparative advantage could make a crucial difference to the prospects for India's balance of payments. It focusses on how resources for greater investment in social sectors—particularly health and education—can be generated by substantially raising their literacy rates and healthcare reforms.

Chapter 5 focusses on the role of 'The Public Sector' in India. Soon after Independence, the public sector was regarded as the principal instrument for raising the level of savings and growth in the economy. Investment rates were low at the time (10 per cent in 1950–51), and the private sector did not have the financial means or technological capacity to undertake large, new investments in industry and infrastructure. The role of the public sector changed dramatically over time, and by 1988–89, it accounted for half the domestic output (at factor cost) in mining, manufacturing, electricity, construction, banking and insurance. However, despite substantial growth in public expenditure, there was no financial accountability or pressure to generate profits. The government became the sole source of funds for investment and the sole arbiter of how public-sector resources were to be used. As the sector became more politicized and controlled, it also became financially unviable and a drain on the national and state budgets.

Over time, action was taken by the government to privatize some loss-making, public-sector enterprises without hurting the interests of consumers and workers. It is important to ensure that the disinvestment process is fair and transparent, and public perceptions of political interference and favouritism are avoided. With a strong independent agency in place to oversee disinvestments, actual implementation can be largely decentralized. Another important priority is to reduce the managerial role of the government in enterprises which are yielding adequate returns on capital. The government should also relinquish completely the powers to appoint chief executives or senior managers of a corporation. Such appointments may be left to an independent agency such as the Union Public Service Commission (UPSC). The government should set standards of service, monitor performance of public enterprises and ensure access to the poor. A reduction in the role of the public sector in the economy is also desirable.

Chapter 6 in Section 2 is on 'Goods and Services'. In recent years, there has been a phenomenal change in the conventional view of services and their role in the economy. The development of certain services is now regarded as one of the preconditions for economic growth, and not as one of its consequences. The boundary between goods and services is also fading, as services of various kinds are delinked from the manufacturing process and are essential elements of the productive structure. Many industrial products are not only manufactured, but also designed, marketed, advertised, distributed, leased and serviced. A significant and rising part of the value added by manufacturers now consists of services.

This chapter deals in detail with macroeconomic policies, particularly fiscal, financial and tariff policies, which have important implications for the development of goods and services to increase growth and employment in the economy. Today, these policies have become more growth-oriented and less inward-looking. Experts are supported through a further reduction of tariffs on goods and services, and equalization of effective rates across sectors. India now has the industrial and entrepreneurial base to break away decisively from the industrial stagnation of the earlier decades. The recent changes in IT, trade patterns and structure of capital flows are also favourable to India. A sustained growth rate of 8–10 per cent per annum in goods and services is achievable and must be the goal of India's economic policy in the future.

This chapter also has a special section on state intervention in all aspects of production and distribution of agricultural commodities. Agricultural growth is not only vital for the economy, but also central to the welfare of the bulk of India's population. Agriculture accounts for about 65 per cent of the country's employment (according to 2016 figures). Rural population (percentage of total population) in

India was reported at 65.07 per cent in 2020.[1] Agricultural growth rates, however, have been significantly lower than the growth rate of the economy as a whole. As a result, the disparity between per capita incomes in agriculture and other sectors has accentuated over the years. This chapter outlines a number of issues which need to be tackled to improve agricultural growth and income of farmers over time. If agricultural growth can be significantly increased, India's national income can grow by 7–8 per cent per annum in the long run, which will make a major dent in the problem of poverty in India.

The last chapter in Section 2 is titled 'Finance and Development: Which Way Now?'. Soon after the liberalization of the economy in 1991, India witnessed a fundamental change in the role of the financial system in the economy. One of the main reasons for this change can be attributed to the transformative roles of the government and the public sector in the allocation of the nation's savings for development. The chapter discusses in detail the shifting paradigm of finance and development and how it has affected the past, present and future of the nation.

Section 3 on 'Politics' has three chapters: 'The Politics of Power' (Chapter 8), 'Political Opportunism' (Chapter 9) and 'Politics and Economics' (Chapter 10). It is well known that politicians, as representatives of the people, enjoy a great deal of power in all spheres of public life. This,

---

[1]The World Bank, https://data.worldbank.org/indicator/SP.RUR.TOTL.ZS?locations=IN. Accessed on 31 March 2022.

after all, is the essence of democracy. The government is expected to work in the interest of the people, and it is their representatives who have to ensure that. Unfortunately, this proposition, which is entirely valid in theory, has become highly vitiated in practice. For example, individual ministers in different ministries are fully empowered to change tax concessions or tax rates (with the pro forma approval of Parliament and the cabinet), or to change educational or urban development policy (with or without the cabinet's approval). The enormous discretionary powers available to politicians at different levels of society, has had several unintended consequences including diversion of resources for the benefit of the better-off sections of society at the expense of the economically backward.

Chapter 8 highlights the fact that the organizational structure of political power is 'pyramidal' in structure. It is wide at the base or the grassroots, where the number of persons elected to political offices, such as the gram panchayats, is large in number and entry is relatively free. However, the number of such offices shrinks drastically at the district, state or Union levels. The size of the electorate increases exponentially as one moves up the ladder, while the number of political constituencies and offices become fewer. The higher the level of an office, the greater the mismatch between supply and demand for that office and increases its scarcity value owing to the pyramidal structure of political power. The scope of powers available to political leaders increases enormously at the state and central levels. This chapter also discusses some issues of importance with respect to the centralization of political power and public dissavings.

Chapter 9 is on 'Political Opportunism,' which is a commonly used euphemism in the literature on behavioural economics to describe the bias among elected representatives at different levels to divest resources under a government programme to their own villages, constituencies or states. The cost of such preferential treatment for society as a whole can be substantial in view of the paucity of resources available under a particular programme. Over time, while the number of all kinds of programmes has increased phenomenally, fiscal resources to finance such programmes have become more stringent at the Centre as well as practically all the states. Political leaders and ministers have virtually unlimited powers to announce new schemes and programmes, or replace and redesignate old programmes. However, they have no room available to implement these programmes because of vast amounts squandered on existing poorly planned programmes.

The pyramidal structure of political power has resulted in the over-centralization of administration rather than its decentralization. This has substantially increased the number of agencies, both horizontally and vertically, in the decision-making process, leading to administrative delays and lack of accountability for non-performance. It is this immense commercial power in the hands of political leaders that makes India different from other mature democracies.

Chapter 10 suggests a few core changes that are practical and pragmatic, and can help bridge the gap between politics and economics so that India can realize its full potential for benefit of all its people. An important priority for the future is to further reduce the political role of the government in the economy. The government should ensure a stable and competitive environment with a strong external sector and a transparent domestic financial system. Since India's balance-of-payments system is now strong, it is desirable to adopt an aggressive 'open economy' policy with as low a level of protection as most competitive economies in the world. Open competition is the most effective deterrent to the emergence of monopolistic practices and monopoly rents.

At the same time, the political role of the government in ensuring the availability of public goods (such as roads or water) and essential services (such as health and education) in the economy must expand substantially. A related political imperative is the need for a joint agreement between leaders of political parties and the trade unions of government employees to improve the economic services of the State. Such an agreement to improve services to the people should be possible through a democratic process. A vital political imperative for the future is also to reduce the role of small parties in Parliament and legislatures and their influence in determining the government's economic agenda.

Section 1

ECONOMY

1

CURRENT SITUATION AND FUTURE PROSPECTS

There is no doubt that India's economy is on a new growth trajectory. Part of the reason for the resurgence of confidence in India's future is the implementation of economic reforms initiated in 1991 and the emergence of a majority-party government in 2014—for the first time since then. With a majority-party government in power, introducing politically difficult economic reforms to reduce poverty and accelerate growth as well as promoting cooperative federalism between the Centre and the states become easier. The sources of comparative advantage of nations are also vastly different today than was the case 50 or even 20 years ago. There are very few developing countries that are as well placed as India to take advantage of the phenomenal changes that have occurred in production technologies, international trade, capital movement and deployment of skilled manpower.

In the past, developing countries were primarily producers of commodities (such as jute, rubber, tea and cotton) and the value added in manufacturing was largely captured by industrial countries. This is no longer the scenario. Developing countries have emerged as major and competitive producers of manufactured products. Consider, for example, the following developments.

Low- and middle-income countries now account for almost 80 per cent of the world's industrial workforce. Even more striking is the fact that, contrary to conventional thinking, the developing countries' share of the world's skilled workforce also jumped from a third to nearly a half. Thus, the industrialized countries no longer have a monopoly on manufacturing production, and developing countries are no longer exclusively dependent on low-value trade in primary products.

The rapid growth in manufacturing has been associated with a high rate of increase in employment and workers' wages. For example, manufacturing wages rose by 270 per cent in real terms between 1970 and 2000, while manufacturing employment increased by 500 per cent during the period of sustained high growth in East Asia.

Such growth has resulted in the movement of workers from low-wage agriculture and plantations to high-wage manufacturing jobs. In the early years of industrialization in developing countries, wage employment tripled between 1957 and 2000, while the share of the workforce employed in agriculture fell from 58 per cent to 26 per cent during the same period.

Earlier, it was believed that the private sector lacked the resources for large-scale, capital-intensive industry. In the past four decades, however, the bulk of investment in infrastructure as well as in capital-intensive and long-gestation projects in developing countries has come from the private, not the public sector.

Several factors explain why the developing countries, in the present phase of the world economy, have emerged as major producers and exporters of manufactured goods. First and foremost, the end of colonial rule and participation by developing countries in the post-war trade negotiations have significantly levelled the international playing fields. Unlike the earlier periods of globalization in the late nineteenth and the early twentieth centuries, the current trading patterns among different groups of countries, with some exceptions, reflect the real comparative advantages of nations. During the early years of the post-colonial period, interventionist strategies in several developing countries helped them establish industrial bases and industrial cultures, which enabled them to exploit the new opportunities in international trade that arose in the last four decades. This process was helped enormously by changes in the direction of foreign investment. Up until the end of World War II (1945), foreign investment was entirely directed towards the production and trade of primary products (for example, plantations, minerals and oil). In more recent years, the bulk of foreign investment has gone into the manufacturing and service industries.

Another crucial factor that has promoted manufacturing trade in developing countries is the cost reduction accompanying technological progress during the last four decades. Technological changes have made the accumulation of skills a more important factor in determining comparative advantage than capital endowments. Developing countries that have benefitted the most from technological changes are those where the levels of literacy and skill development have been high—East Asia and China earlier, and India now. Finally, the sharp decline in costs of communications and transport has made geography and the proximity to markets less relevant in influencing the choice of location for manufacturing industries.

The aforementioned changes have enabled developing countries to play a more decisive role in international trade. The extent to which a country or region has benefited from these trends has, of course, depended upon its policies and overall economic performance. Initial endowments and conditions (particularly with respect to literacy and health) have played a crucial role, but these too are subject to change.

As a result of conscious policy choices, India did not benefit greatly from the growth of the developing world's trade in manufacturing until lately. In fact, India's share of world trade fell from about 2 per cent in 1950 to only 0.5–0.6 per cent in the 1990s. In the current scenario, India is perhaps better situated to take advantage of sweeping technological changes than most other developing countries, including China. We had the advantage of a head start in industrialization and in providing broad-based opportunities in skill-based education, including technological and managerial education. It can only be a matter of speculation to ascertain the extent to which India would have been better off economically had it seized its initial advantages to capture skills-related value-addition opportunities in manufacturing in the earlier decades.

In recent years, an even more phenomenal change from India's point of view is the growing role of skills-based services in determining the comparative advantage of economies. The development of certain services is now considered as one of the preconditions for economic growth, and not as one of its consequences. The boundary between goods and services is also gradually disappearing, as services of various kinds are delinked from the manufacturing process and have become essential elements of the productive structure.

The change in the role of services has been brought about by unprecedented and unforeseen advances in computer and communication technology in the last four decades. An important aspect of the 'services revolution' is that geography and levels of industrialization are no longer the primary determinants of the location of facilities for the production of services. As a result, the traditional role of developing countries is also changing—from mere recipients to important providers of long-distance services. India, too, has participated in this changing scenario, and exports of certain services (for example, software) are expanding faster than the overall trade. The potential for expansion of jobs and incomes in the services sector is truly immense. From India's point of view, some of the recent global developments which provide opportunities for substantial growth are the following:

i. The fastest-growing segment of services is knowledge-based, such as professional and technical services, particularly in IT. India has a tremendous advantage in the supply of such services because of the highly developed structure of technological and educational institutions, and lower labour costs.
ii. Progress in IT is making it increasingly possible to unbundle the production and consumption of information-intensive service activities. These activities—research and development (R&D), computing, inventory management, quality control, accounting, personnel administration, clerical services, marketing, advertising, distribution and legal services—are performed in all economic sectors. They play a fundamental role not only in service industries, but also in manufacturing and primary industries. With progress in the field of IT, outsourcing of these activities has become feasible.
iii. Unlike most other prices, world prices of transport and communication services have fallen dramatically. By 1960, sea transport costs were less than a third of their 1920 level, and they have continued to plummet. The cost of a telephone call fell tenfold between 1970 and 2000. Moreover, the cost of communication is also becoming independent of distance and networks are becoming more international. The most dramatic example in this area is provided by the Internet, which now links millions of computers across the world. Many large corporations are also building

dedicated international networks to meet their global communication needs. India's geographical distance from several important industrial markets (for instance, North America) is no longer an issue in the cost structure of skills-based services.

iv. Technological innovation is expanding opportunities for services to be embodied in goods that are traded internationally. In other words, India does not necessarily have to be a low-cost producer of certain types of goods (such as computers or discs) before it can become an efficient supplier of services embodied in them (such as software or music). It is possible now to provide value-added services without waiting to 'catch up' in technology for the production of sophisticated equipment or products.

v. Along with incomes and employment, there is a structural shift in the pattern of demand in industrial countries in favour of services. The decline in the share of manufacturing in the output of rich countries implies a relative decline in their demand for industrial raw materials and fuels. This means that in the future, the growth in exports of developing countries will depend less on natural resource endowments and more on efficiency in providing services and service-intensive goods.

There is now a new category of products in the international trade, known as the 'new' manufactured products. This category includes major electronic products of automatic data-processing and telecommunications, semi-conductor devices and electronics microcircuits. What is striking is the rising share of developing countries in the export of these highly sophisticated products. By 2000, developing countries' share in new-product exports had risen to 28 per cent (from 11.5 per cent in 1980). This was significantly higher than their share of 22 per cent in the world's manufactured exports.

In light of these developments in production and trade in new products and services, it is clear that the expansion of high-technology and knowledge-based services must have an important role in any strategy for rapid growth of incomes and jobs in India in the twenty-first century.

Fortunately, there are very few developing countries that are as well placed as India to take advantage of the phenomenal changes that have occurred in production technologies, international trade, movement and deployment of skilled manpower. The shift in India's comparative advantage has substantial implications for India's growth potential. If the growth performance of the Indian economy can be further accelerated and sustained at the level of 8–9 per cent per annum over the next 25 years, extreme poverty in India can be virtually eradicated. The higher the growth of the economy, the greater will be the capacity of the government to finance expenditure for essential social services. The combination of higher government expenditure on the provision of social services with higher growth in employment opportunities can have a decisive impact on poverty levels.

It is no coincidence that countries and regions that have

registered high and sustained growth rates over a reasonable period of time are also the ones that have achieved the best results in reducing poverty and improving the health and nutrition of their people. In some cases, progress in reducing poverty or improving the level of human development indicators has been much greater than would seem warranted by their rate of growth, as has happened in the Indian state of Kerala, and in Sri Lanka. Unfortunately, there are also cases where high growth has been combined with a worsening of the poverty ratio (for example, Brazil in the 1970s), or where high per capita income has not resulted in adequate progress in education and other social services (for instance, some of the oil-rich countries). However, such cases are nothing more than exceptions, with valid reasons behind them. Over time, it became clear that Sri Lanka and Kerala made commendable progress in poverty alleviation in the past, albeit with low growth, but are now finding it difficult to sustain the process. Owing to fiscal stringency, per capita expenditures on anti-poverty programmes have also suffered a decline. Unemployment has become pervasive as a consequence of low industrial growth. This impedes further progress on the poverty alleviation front.

On any global indicator of socio-economic well-being—be it adult literacy, infant mortality, maternal mortality, life expectancy or gender bias—India's performance remains among the bottom one-third. What is worse is that progress in all these areas is much slower than in other developing countries (aside from the least-developed ones). There are multiple causes for the persistent poverty in India. There are problems of governance, widespread administrative apathy and rampant corruption in the exercise of state power. Governments—at the Centre, in the states and at the local levels—are heavily debt ridden and virtually without means to care adequately for the poor.

If the Indian economy can sustain a growth rate of 8–9 per cent in the next 25 years, our per capita gross domestic product (GDP) will double in eight to nine years. Even if employment elasticity is significantly less than unity, new jobs will be created at a rate that is substantially higher than the growth of labour force. Real wages are likely to rise at a rate that is at least as high as per capita income, if not higher. This has, in fact, been the experience of several fast-growing countries. In light of India's participatory social and political environment, there is no reason why the same could not happen here. If state governments reduce their public debt by reducing their debt-financed assets in the public sector, the interest burden can be reduced significantly. This will release resources for greater investment in social sectors, particularly health and education. It is interesting to note that countries and regions that have succeeded in substantially raising their literacy rates are also those that have succeeded in alleviating poverty.

The above may be too optimistic a view. Without doubt, even after the favourable changes in the economic policy environment, there is a need to improve the overall policy framework and enhance the efficiency with which resources are used. With years of neglect, the physical infrastructure, particularly that of transport (i.e. roads, ports and railways), is in bad shape. Similarly, unless investment in energy picks up, large parts of the country will face acute shortages of power in the near future.

A lot, therefore, remains to be done before India is able to exploit new opportunities or realize its full potential. However, the important point is that these opportunities are there, and that the patterns of global trade and investment have changed in India's favour. The only constraint on our country's economic future is the lack of a strong political will to move ahead decisively to overcome the shortcomings in the policies and administrative practices of the past. It is to be hoped that such a consensus will emerge, and India can take its rightful place as one of the leading economies in the world in the twenty-first century.

2

SCIENCE AND DEVELOPMENT

Economic growth is the result of both slow and steady improvements in technology and the knowledge embodied in physical and human capital as well as from the 'breakthrough' inventions. Breakthrough inventions are, however, unpredictable and may at times change the direction of the entire industrial structure.

This chapter briefly addresses some of the questions that concern all of us: what is the relation between science and technology? How do they influence the growth trajectories of the world economy and the well-being of people? What should be the relative roles of the state and market in ensuring the blooming of scientific knowledge and its culmination into technological know-how? What do successful country experiences teach us in this regard?

Relation between Science and Technology: Invention, Innovation and Diffusion

From an economist's viewpoint, the relation between science and technology reminds one immediately of the great twentieth-century Austrian economist Joseph Alois Schumpeter. Schumpeter made a fundamental distinction between invention, which is the discovery of new techniques, and innovation, which consists of the practical application of an invention in production for the market.[1] Invention is performed by the inventor while innovation is the task of the entrepreneur.

The classic example of this is perhaps the eighteenth-century industrial revolution in Britain. The progress of Britain at that time did not lie merely in the invention of scientific tools, which was primitive by modern standards but also in its commercial adoption. Thus, James Watt is not only remembered as the inventor of the steam engine but also as one who put it to commercial use. It is this commercial adoption that Schumpeter referred to as 'innovation'. Many of the inventors of modern software, too, fall in this combined category of inventor-innovator rolled into one. Often, the entities of innovator and inventor are distinct, and thus, it is the intimate interlink between invention and innovation that marks the interrelationship between science and technology.

In Schumpeter's analytical structure, there is a third stage

---

[1]Schumpeter, Joseph A., *Capitalism, Socialism and Democracy,* HarperCollins, New York, 1995.

of the twin process of invention-innovation, viz. diffusion, which occurs only when the scientist and the entrepreneur join hands. The invention and initial innovation of any product or process may be the property or outcome of an individual or company effort. But how are they made popular? What ensures their cost reduction and universal adoption? It is only through proper diffusion of the scientific knowledge embodied in the marketable form of a particular product or process that it gets universalized. Technological history is full of examples of such diffusions, or knowledge spill overs.

Once the interlinkage between science and technology is recognized as the prime force behind economic progress, it is also necessary to consider the optimal mode of interplay between them. Put differently, often the question arises: what kind of research is more necessary—pure or applied? The issue becomes all the more important in the context of funding science programmes. However, like many of the fundamental choice problems of human life, there is no standard model that can be universally pursued.

At a conceptual level, nevertheless, one can have a two-way classification of the agencies involved with scientific research, viz. knowledge-generation agencies and knowledge-application/diffusion agencies. While the former includes universities or technical schools, big scientific national networks or various research corporations are examples of the latter. A related question would be: what kind of research should have greater priority? Would the research paradigm of the scientific pursuit be dictated solely by utilitarian consideration and accordingly subjected to social controls?

All economies in the world faced this dilemma at some time or the other. In fact, the issue can be traced back to a public debate that took place in Great Britain during the 1930s between two experts: Michael Polanyi and J.D. Bernal. While the former stressed the need for autonomy and self-governance for the scientific community, the latter expressed his preference in favour of societal and government regulation over research agenda. Thus, often one finds a tension between what is called an 'open' science and an 'appropriable' science.

Such dichotomy often arises from a confusion between private and social rate of return of scientific pursuit. The immediate social rate of return out of an otherwise esoteric research programme may be low, but in the longer run, it could have the potential of being appropriable. The contribution to science and technology comes from both these two kinds of research, and often the degrees of success in the field of technical capabilities depend on the degree of cohesion between these two kinds of scientific paradigms.

In this regard, it may be noted that in many fields of today's world of scientific research, such as modern biology, the distinction between basic and applied science is increasingly getting blurred. In that respect, knowledge-based research can be classified into three categories: (a) fundamental research; (b) basic industrial research; and (c) applied R&D. India needs all the three kinds of research and needs to make an endeavour to maintain a symbiotic relation between them.

Impact of Science and Technology on Development

Enhanced labour, capital and technical progress are the three principal sources of economic growth of nations. The distinction between capital and technical progress is often a matter of degree. While an increase in capital is interpreted as the quantitative change in the existing capital stock of any country, technical progress refers to qualitative changes in the production technique. However, the term 'capital' needs to be taken in a rather broad sense, so that it encompasses three distinct kinds of capital: physical, financial and human. Accordingly, the domain of the concept 'technical progress' gets extended to all these three kinds of capital. This basic broad definition of capital is central to the understanding of the impact of science and technology on economic well-being. Moreover, the contribution of science and technology on economic growth comes both in the form of capital and technical progress.

The process through which these technological innovations get transmitted to higher growth trajectory has been described by Schumpeter as one of creative destruction. In his words:

> The fundamental impulse that sets and keeps the capitalist engine in motion comes from the new goods, the new methods of production or transportation, the new markets, the new form of industrial organization

> the capitalist enterprise creates... (These) illustrate the same process of industrial mutation that incessantly revolutionizes the economic structure from within, incessantly destroying the old one, incessantly creating a new one. This process of Creative Destruction is the essential fact about capitalism.[2]

Recent theories of endogenous growth stress two facts of innovation. First, it is the engine of growth, and second, it is endogenously generated by competitive profit-seeking firms. The key feature of the process is that knowledge acts as a public good and creates economy-wide increasing returns. The public stock of knowledge that has accumulated from the spill over of the previous inventions is a crucial input in the technology to generate new ideas. While the rate of knowledge obsolescence rose towards the end of the twentieth century, the rate of knowledge diffusion was even faster.

An important issue governing the impact of science and technology on the well-being of a nation is the employment potential of any technology. An oft-expressed fear associated with the emergence of any technological innovation is that it is labour-displacing. The crucial issue in this context is the employment elasticity of an innovation-induced growth. Though the innovation of a new technology may be labour-saving per se, the development of ancillaries or related products may give rise to newer employment opportunities; it is the net employment absorption that determines the employment elasticity of growth.

---

[2]Ibid.

There is strong evidence to suggest that so long as technology helps to widen the resource base of the production system of the economy, there is no a priori reason for technological innovation to be employment reducing in an aggregate sense. The East Asian example is a case worth considering on this issue. It is now widely accepted that notwithstanding the proportions of factor utilization of any production process, there has to be ample emphasis on labour for ensuring the welfare of the working class. East Asian governments used many such policies: land reform in Korea and Taiwan, housing subsidies in Hong Kong and Singapore, and credit targeting for small businesses and investments in rural infrastructure in Indonesia and Malaysia. Accordingly, despite the varied degrees of tolerance by their labour unions, wages increased as fast as GDP and unemployment declined in all of the East Asian countries.

Policy Framework to Foster Innovation and Technology Development

International experience is full of success stories about different kinds of innovation. In fact, internationally, there are four different forms of technology transfer, viz:

i. Acquisition of a share of the equity of the technology-producing firm;
ii. Licence agreement;
iii. Outright purchase of equipment, know-how or blue print;
iv. Flow of human resources.

There are success stories in all these modes of technology upgradation. For example, countries like Japan acquired patents from outside, and then took recourse to their indigenous assimilation and further development so as to finally export them.

Similarly, many of the high-growth East Asian countries have little original technological inventions—bulk of the technological capabilities came from licencing agreements or direct foreign investment. Technological activity in developing countries tends to be almost of the 'incremental type' rather than of 'Schumpeterian-frontier-moving-type'. Numerous case studies of such experiments can be cited from the Indian experience. Some examples include adopting imported designs of power plant equipment to suit local quality of coal and changes in the designs of tractors, vehicles and a variety of consumer durables to suit local conditions of production of components.

It must, however, be recognized that success stories of 'in-country research' leading to output growth are exceptions rather than the rule. The time lag between 'effort' and 'results' in any innovation activity is normally large. An economy has to afford it. And an economy that is pursuing a pattern of investment (such as infrastructure development) where projects have long gestation periods may not find it very easy to allocate large resources to innovative activities where gestation lags are even larger than these infrastructure projects. Besides, there are risks associated with innovation effort.

Looking at science and technology in the context of its

contribution to production of goods and provision of services to the people, the objective is maximization of output. If the needs of the society are to be fulfilled at the lowest cost, the 'make' versus 'buy' issues become important, i.e. the trade option has to be kept in view. While the commodity markets may tend to be 'perfect', technology markets, even if they exist, are characterized by their 'imperfectness' marked by inadequate information and exclusive rights acquired through patents or otherwise.

India is frequently compelled to acquire technology through imports. Firms trade in 'technology' not as a commodity but as a 'perceived' economic advantage for a stream of returns in the future. International political considerations cannot be ruled out in technology trade. Licencing by governments of developed countries is a common feature. However, when it comes to bargaining regarding technology transfer, the issue of indigenous availability often becomes extremely important. For example, it has been observed in India that the prices quoted by foreign firms for capital goods and equipment drop when a distinct alternative supply possibility emerges. This has been the experience in a number of industries like electric power equipment, telephone exchange equipment and machine tools.

There are two fundamental issues that are central to any policy governing science and technology. First, what is the funding process of innovation activities? Second, if the diffusion for technological innovation is indeed fast, what is the incentive for the innovator? Often, there is a wedge between the commercial successes of a new innovation and the profits appropriated by the innovator—the problem becomes all the more important in view of the fact that in a number of cases, the innovative activity has substantial fixed cost. A number of solutions are practised in different degrees in various countries. Use of subsidies or tax concessions for R&D expenditure, adoption of cooperative R&D venture and national champions, and detailed patent laws are the major policy instruments adopted in this regard.

So far as funding of R&D expenditure is concerned, considerable differences exist even among the advanced economics. Public expenditure on technology development for civilian industrial application accounts for a small share of public R&D budgets in the industrial economies. Interestingly, a number of studies have found that the effects of direct government funding on the productivity performance of the recipient firms are smaller than privately financed R&D investment. India spends roughly 0.7 per cent of its GDP on R&D. Furthermore, it was observed that the ratio had shown remarkable stability over the years. However, it needs to be noted that these statistics cover only those industrial units who chose to get registered with the Department of Scientific and Industrial Research (DSIR).

Considering the fact that over time, there had been substantial reduction in the number of units registered with the DSIR, some underestimation is indicated in these numbers. Interestingly, out of a relatively small amount of R&D spending, more than three-fourths comes from the government; thus the possibility of underestimating R&D expenditure could be present only in the remaining one-fourth.

Financing of innovative activities with private-sector initiative is indeed problematic. Gone are the days when individual entrepreneurs were capable of financing uncertain and risky technological innovations which have much profitable potential. On the other hand, stock markets also may not be forthcoming in financing these high-growth but risky ventures. To resolve this constraint, 'venture capital' comes in, which is essentially equity investment in companies that are not mature enough to get access to capital market but have high-growth potentials to compensate for the uncertainties inherent in such ventures. There are a number of success stories of such venture capital financing in the developed world; successful corporations like Apple Computers or Genetech, which produces bio-medical products would not have been born without active venture capital participation.

The guidelines on 'venture capital' issued by the Reserve Bank of India (RBI) in 1988 recognized their role in the Indian conditions. A number of venture capital institutions came up in due course—the Technology Development and Investment Corporation of India (set up by ICICI), Technology Development Fund (set up by IDBI) and Equity Development Scheme (set up by SBI Caps and Canara Bank), to name a few. The number of active members of the Indian Venture and Alternate Capital Association (IVCA) and the investments by venture capital funds, have also gone up substantially. However, despite this growth, India still has a long way to go in the field of venture capital.

Contributions of the Council of Scientific and Industrial Research

In the context of the efficiency of the invention-innovation process, the role of the Council of Scientific and Industrial Research (CSIR) is of paramount importance. Much has been written on the strengths and weaknesses of the CSIR. In this context, the 1986 Report of CSIR Review Committee (Chairman: Abid Hussain) is particularly interesting. The report found that the presence of multiple objectives, suboptimal scale of operation, lack of sustained and meaningful interaction between the CSIR and its actual and potential users, and lack of suitable incentive support had, in the past, limited the usefulness of the CSIR in the Indian economy. Nevertheless, there were exogenous factors, beyond the control of such scientific institutions that were responsible for its limited usefulness. Lack of industry support and a regulatory regime had hindered its proper functioning. Often, the reasons for lack of smooth functioning of institutions like the CSIR were interactive and, consequently the responsibility became collective. In the future, the objectives of such science–technology interaction would be a proper blend of different situation-specific modes, like technology missions, technology programmes, sponsored research, basic research and societal science programmes.

In this context, it is encouraging that CSIR also issued a white paper, *CSIR 2001: Vision and Strategy.* Among other things, it set up the goal to achieve self-sufficiency in financing primarily through development of some niche areas in globally competitive technologies, holding of patent bank and releasing 10 per cent of operational expenditure from intellectual property licencing. Moreover, as a strategy for achieving these goals, it called for development of an effective marketing system and adoption of a stimulating intellectual property-oriented outlook.

As part of the reform policies for the industrial sector, in July 1991, a policy for technology transfer was also introduced. Automatic approval for foreign technological agreement to high-priority industries up to a specified amount was granted. Automatic approval was also granted to other industries provided they did not require the spending of free foreign exchange. For hiring foreign technicians and foreign testing of indigenously developed technologies, all prior clearances were done away with.

The government, apart from giving a number of tax concessions for R&D purposes, also took a number of policy measures with far-reaching significance in the field of science and technology. A Technology Development Board was established in 1996 with a threefold strategy, viz: (i) facilitating the development of new technologies; (ii) assimilation and adaptation of imported technologies; and (iii) providing catalytic support to industries and R&D institutions to work together.

The Five-Year Plans emphasized the role of science and

technology in the development process to a great extent and proposed the adoption of a multifaceted approach. Among the specific issues raised in the plan documents are:

i. Creation of a conducive environment in R&D institutions for minimizing hierarchical bureaucracy;
ii. Emphasis on human resource development and motivation as elements of qualitative growth, as well as maintenance of a proper balance between fundamental research and applied research;
iii. Development of a 'consortia approach' in which one of the scientific laboratories acting as a nodal institution forms a consortium with industry and other departments; and
iv. Effective implementation of science and technology for societal development.

Realization of this vision through adoption of operationally viable strategies has gone a long way in enhancing Indian technological capabilities.

Conclusion

It is now 75 years since India gained independence from British colonial rule. In these years, India's achievements in the arena of scientific pursuit—material and intellectual—have been phenomenal. Although there is still scope for improvement in the policy and legal sphere, the directional indications are right. A fairly liberal environment must be created where ideas of science and technology can bloom and be transcreated into innovative ventures by entrepreneurs. For a nation that aspires to be at the forefront of the technological revolution that is taking place in the new sectors of growth in the global economy, there is certainly no dearth of talent, skills and the resources to achieve the dream. The scientific, industrial and financial communities need to come together to make it possible for young men and women to take maximum advantage of the opportunities that lie ahead.

3

INFORMATION TECHNOLOGY AND BANKING

It goes without saying that the two sectors of the economy—IT and banking—are vital for India's growth and broad-based development. There is also a tremendous mutuality of interest in these two sectors. In the banking sector, IT can reduce costs, increase volumes and facilitate customized financial products. Similarly, IT requires banking and financial services to facilitate its growth. In other words, financial services need IT, and IT needs financial services to make the maximum impact.

The changes brought out by new developments in IT are truly revolutionary. An interesting question is: why now? Computers have been around for a long time and while the Internet, in its present form, is of relatively recent origin, other forms of fast global communications, particularly telephones and faxes, have also been around for quite a while. Why is it that only recently IT has become not only an instrument of communication and information, but also such an important contributor to growth and productivity?

The revolution in new technology has helped three other important global economic developments since the 1990s. The first is the declining importance of manufacturing and the increasing importance of value-added services as a source of income and growth. In industrial countries, the share of manufacturing in the total national income has declined sharply over the years to less than 20 per cent. In developing countries like India too, value-added services, such as transport, communication, banking, construction, management, marketing and administration are growing in proportion to national income. In our country, the contribution of services to national income is more than 50 per cent annually. Interestingly, the fastest-growing segment in the manufacturing sector is also connected with services, e.g. data processing equipment, semi-conductor devices and so on. Interestingly, 'services' are generally more conducive to IT inputs in terms of quality and costs than manufacturing. In banking, for example, entire transactions, including delivery, can be conducted over the Internet. This is not possible in respect of say, steel or clothing.

Second, in recent years, there has been a substantial lowering of barriers to trade and capital mobility, the so-called 'globalization process'. If quantitative restrictions on trade and tariffs had remained high, it is obvious that the global advantage that the Internet has conferred in respect of trade or commerce would have been substantially less.

Greater openness has contributed to the tremendous growth of market for IT, just as IT has helped in accelerating the globalization process. As a result, distance is no longer crucial and geographical location is no longer a key to business decisions. Companies are likely to locate anywhere in the world where they can find the best skills and the best 'time zone' advantage.

The third crucial factor, which is related to the second, is the growing integration of developing countries' financial markets with those of the developed countries' financial markets, including equity markets. Developments in Nasdaq, for example, or Dow Jones have a worldwide impact. In countries in different time zones, this integration has increased the importance of timely information, and therefore, of IT and information providers and analysts.

Interestingly, all the above developments, which have contributed to the IT revolution, are also to India's advantage. India has been able to take advantage of IT because of its 'skills' endowments. The increasing importance of the services revolution and the decreasing importance of distance in defining comparative advantage have meant that it is now possible to unbundle the production and consumption of various types of services across the globe. This means that India does not necessarily have to be a low-cost producer of certain types of goods (e.g. computer or discs) to become an efficient supplier of services embodied in them (e.g. software or music).

Similarly, freer capital mobility has meant that capital is no longer a binding constraint to development. Capital is available in plenty and any capital-deficit developing country or, for that matter, any corporate entity, can attract capital to carry on value-added economic activity. Among developing countries, despite much inefficiency, India has one of the better financial institutional infrastructures, including one of the oldest equity markets in the world. Most of the financial practices and accounting standards also meet the test of international acceptance. Globalization of financial services has provided substantial opportunities for export of software as well as management expertise from India to even the most sophisticated markets in the world.

Some of these factors mentioned above emphasize the two-way relationship between technology and global macroeconomic developments. India has benefited from these global developments in the '90s because it has also adjusted domestic policies to take advantage of the new economy and new developments in trade, capital and finance. It is important to emphasize that technology is not sufficient by and of itself to generate growth or bring about economic prosperity. It can contribute most when the economic environment and macroeconomic policies are conducive to its inputs. Accelerating the momentum of economic reform and institutional innovations in the economy are major future challenges for India to take maximum advantage of these new trends.

Nowhere is this more important than in the banking and the financial sector. India cannot benefit from IT as much as it can, and should, unless it transforms the way it does banking business. There are some specific characteristics of money and finance which make it particularly amenable to benefit from IT, provided we seize the new opportunities. Among these are:

i. As mentioned earlier, unlike most other goods and services, money and finance can actually be used, transferred and delivered electronically. In other words, no physical movement or physical delivery is required to complete transactions and their end use. This explains why financial volumes, with the aid of electronics and computerization, have grown phenomenally in recent years. Total financial transactions in a day can exceed the entire GDP of an industrial country.

ii. In the financial sector, credits and debits need to be settled in real time so that the value risk and default risk are minimized. Earlier, when payment and settlement system was based on movements of papers, it used to take several days to reconcile debits and credits. Today, payment and settlement system can happen on a real-time basis.

iii. A related characteristic is that, with the possibility of payment and settlement taking place simultaneously in real time, risks and uncertainties can be reduced. This also reduces the cost of capital. This has tremendous advantages for increasing productivity and generating higher output at lower cost. Information Technology has also made it possible to devise complex financial products, such as derivatives, without adding to risk or uncertainty,

> which, in turn, has expanded the scope for meeting various kinds of financial preferences, risk profiles and different requirements of savers and investors.

These characteristics represent a tremendous advantage for growth of IT in finance. There are, however, certain limitations also in respect of financial transactions compared with e-commerce in physical products. There is a greater need for supervisory and regulatory system since many financial institutions, such as banks, mutual funds and pension funds, deal with other people's money. It is important to ensure that people's savings are safe and not diverted or misused. Financial system can also be highly 'leveraged'. To safeguard investors' interest, it becomes necessary to impose some limits on leveraging in relation to the size of owned funds. A related requirement is that the total volume of money in the system has to be related to the size of the real economy. In other words, financial agencies, unless specifically authorized to do so, cannot be allowed to create 'new' money. Otherwise, money itself will lose its value and the economy will be characterized by high inflation. Unlike the physical exchange of goods, the financial system also has 'negative externalities'. Instability here can hurt those who do not directly participate as savers or lenders, as happened in East Asia.

The growth of IT has also posed certain special challenges for the banking system. There is a real possibility of disintermediation. There are new opportunities for savers and investors to deal directly with each other rather than through the banking system, unless banks can provide some value addition in terms of return and safety of funds, or investment advice. Banks have to change the old ways of doing things. This poses a challenge, particularly for public-sector banks. The Human Resources Development (HRD), which has been a relatively neglected area in banks, is absolutely crucial. Increasingly, it is the 'people' who contribute to value addition in services rather than 'materials' or fixed assets.

These are some considerations that distinguish financial markets from other markets where IT is going to revolutionize the ways of doing business. What does all this add up to? Increasing use of IT in finance is inevitable and there are going to be more and more transactions taking place across the Internet and the Web. At the same time, much greater supervision, surveillance and regulation of money transactions conducted electronically or over the Web is going to be required. In India, these systems are yet to evolve fully but a beginning has been made by setting up an Indian Financial Network (INFINET) system, an electronic Real-Time Gross Settlement (RTGS) system and faster computerization of bank branches. However, we still have a long way to go. As new methods of supervision evolve, there is also substantial need for legislative changes. The Information Technology Act, 2000 (IT Act) has made an important advance but, over time, new needs will arise.

On the whole, there is no doubt that new opportunities are emerging for India and for knowledge-based industries. At the same time, the deterioration that is taking place in public institutions, including knowledge-based universities, public administration and delivery of public services cannot be ignored. Looking at the long run, the expansion of knowledge-based industries and services, including IT and banking, are not likely to be viable with stagnation and deterioration in public institutional framework. All private and public institutions need to give some consideration to this question. How and in what ways can they, as a group, who are benefiting from the current global trends, contribute to establishing a new collaborative relationship with the country's public administration and public delivery mechanisms?

An equally important task for the future is to improve corporate governance in India. Many companies, particularly in the 'old economy', are still operating in an environment where public trust in their business practices is not very high. Thus, very few people prefer to put their savings deposits with private-sector corporations, however high their market capitalization. Almost half of those who did make their deposits with them complained about not receiving proper service in respect of deposits made by them. It is interesting to note that a majority of the people would rather put their deposits with public-sector financial institutions, even though they pay lower rates of interest. In the future, India's new economy firms would not only become models to emulate but also set the standards and infuse a new culture in management practices in all sectors of the economy.

4

INDIA'S STAND IN THE TWENTY-FIRST CENTURY

During the first 50 years of India's independence, its economic record was relatively poor. Total national income grew by about 4 per cent per annum. Per capita income, or income per head, grew by a meagre 1.9 per cent per annum on an average. As a result, India was seen as one of the poorest countries with a per capita income that was close to the lowest in the world. Unfortunately, India also continues to be near the bottom of the league of nations in terms of most other indicators of human or social development. According to the official count in 1995, nearly one-third of Indians live below the so-called 'poverty line', i.e. their income and consumption are even less than half of India's low average per capita income. Nevertheless, paradoxical as it may seem, in recent years, the patterns of global trade and investment have moved in our favour.

India now has the opportunity and potential to achieve what it could not in the previous 50 or 100 years, i.e. poverty elimination. India's comparative advantage no longer lies in the production of low-value, low-technology and labour-intensive goods, but in relatively high-value, skill-intensive and high-technology products and services.

It is true that foreign trade and investment have a relatively small share in our country's national income and total investment. As such, a faster growth in these components alone cannot dramatically improve the outlook for poverty alleviation. However, a favourable shift in India's comparative advantage can make a crucial difference to the prospects for its balance of payments. Unlike the past, our external trade and payments position need not be a constraint on growth in the twenty-first century, but can become an important source of strength for the economy.

The sources of comparative advantage of nations are vastly different today from what they were 30–40 years ago. For example, 40 years ago, developing countries were primarily producers of commodities such as jute, rubber, tea and cotton and the value added in manufacturing was largely captured by industrial countries. This is no longer true. Developing countries have now emerged as major and competitive producers of manufactured products. As mentioned in the previous chapter, the following developments have subsequently improved the comparative advantage of several developing countries:

i. In the 1990s, low- and middle-income countries accounted for almost 80 per cent of the world's industrial workforce. Among the world's skilled workforce, the share of developing countries increased from one-third to almost half. This signalled an era where the industrialized countries no longer held dominance of manufacturing production.

ii. A fast growth in manufacturing has been associated with nearly 500 per cent increase in employment and wages of workers. The substantial growth in employment has resulted in movement of workers from low-wage agriculture and plantations to high-wage manufacturing jobs.

iii. In the past three decades, however, the bulk of investment in developing countries in infrastructure, and capital-intensive and long-gestation projects has come from the private sector and not the public sector.

A number of factors account for why developing countries, in the present phase of development of the world economy, have emerged as major producers and exporters of manufactured goods. First and foremost, the end of British rule and participation by developing countries in post-War trade negotiations have significantly levelled the international playing field. Interventionist strategies during the early years of the post-colonial period helped establish an industrial base and industrial culture in several developing countries, which could be used to exploit the new opportunities in international trade. Up to the end of the Second World War, foreign investment was entirely directed towards production and trade of primary products (e.g. plantations, minerals and oil). In more recent years, the bulk of foreign investment has gone into manufacturing and service industries. Another important factor which has promoted the growth of developing countries' trade in manufacturing is the cost-reducing technological changes of the last three decades. Technological change has made the accumulation of skills a more important factor in determining comparative advantage than capital endowments.

Owing to conscious policy choices, India did not benefit immensely from the rapid growth that the developing world's trade in manufacturing experienced. In fact, our share of world trade fell from about 2 per cent in 1950 to only 0.5–0.6 per cent in the 1990s. However, India was perhaps better situated to take advantage of sweeping technological changes than most other developing countries, including China. We had the advantage of an early start in industrialization and in providing broad-based opportunities in skill-based education, including technological and managerial education. It can only be a matter of speculation of how much better off India would have been economically if it had seized its initial advantages to capture skills-related value addition in manufacturing.

The 1990s experienced a rather phenomenal change from India's point of view with the ever-increasing role of skill-based services in determining the comparative advantage of economies. Thus, it is imperative that the development of certain services is given more focus as their development is now regarded, not as one of its consequences, but in fact, as one of the preconditions of economic growth. The fine line between goods and services is also disappearing, as services of various kinds are delinked from the manufacturing process and become essential elements of the productive structure.

As mentioned earlier, there is a new category of products circling international trade. This category is referred to as 'new' manufactured products. World exports of these products, which were linked to exports of high value-added services, reached over $360 billion in 1993 compared with $76 billion in 1980. What is equally striking is the rising share of developing countries in the exports of these highly sophisticated products. By 1993, developing countries' share in new-product exports had risen to 28 per cent (from 11.5 per cent in 1980). This was significantly higher than their share of 22 per cent in total world manufactured exports.

If we look at the developments made in production and trade in new products and services, one can decipher that the expansion of high-technology and knowledge-based services must have an important place in any strategy for rapid growth of incomes and jobs in India in the twenty-first century.

Only a handful of developing countries were able to match India to take advantage of the phenomenal changes that have occurred in international trade, production technologies, capital movement and deployment of skilled manpower. A small but telling example of the change in India's position over the last 40 years is that today there are more Indian-origin managers in the city of London than there are British or US managers in Mumbai. India has acquired the knowledge and the skills to build any project, manage any firm and contribute to production and processing of a wide variety of industrial and consumer products. However, there is a major implication affecting India's growth potential with the shift in India's comparative advantage. In fact, from the mid-1980s to the mid-1990s, after nearly 20 years, the industrial production saw an increase of 8.5 per cent per annum on an average. National income also increased in a substantial manner during this period (over 6 per cent per annum as against an average of 3.5 per cent per annum during the period 1950–80). The strong relationship that exists between sustained growth and reduction of poverty is an important conclusion that emerges from the recent economic history of developing countries. The higher the growth of the economy, the greater seems to be the capacity of the government to finance social expenditure. Higher government expenditure on the provision of social services combined with higher growth in employment opportunities (as a result of growth) can make a decisive impact on poverty levels.

It is no coincidence that only those countries were able to achieve the best results in reducing poverty and improving the health and nutrition of their people who have registered high and sustained rates of growth over a reasonable period. In some cases, progress in reducing poverty or improving the level of human development indicators has been much greater than would seem warranted by their rate of growth, as has happened in the Indian state of Kerala, and Sri Lanka. There are also cases where high growth has been combined with a worsening of the poverty ratio or where high per capita incomes have not resulted in adequate progress in education and other social services (e.g. some of the oil-rich countries). However, such cases are not many and they have their own special reasons. Per capita expenditures on anti-poverty programmes have declined because of fiscal stringency. In view of low industrial growth, unemployment has become a pervasive problem. This is now a major obstacle to further progress on the poverty front.

In 1951, when our first Five-Year Plan was launched, it was expected that India's per capita income will double by 1980, and illiteracy and poverty will be practically eliminated. However, only half of this was actually achieved. Per capita income increased by only 50 per cent by 1980. The decline in poverty levels and improvement in other indicators of human deve1opment were also below expectation. In the mid-1990s, India's rank in the Human Development Index (HDI), compiled by the United Nations Development Programme, was 135 among 173 countries globally. The absolute value of the HDI for India was 0.38 compared with 0.89 for Barbados, which ranked first among the developing countries. The HDI for India was close to that of Ghana, Haiti and Nigeria. It was much worse than that of China (0.64), Korea (0.86), Mexico (0.80) and Malaysia (0.79). What was even more striking was that the rate of change in the HDI for India was much slower than that of fast-growing countries. During the three decades from 1965 to 1995, India's HDI increased by only 17 points (from 0.21 in 1960 to 0.38 in 1993). Over the same period, the HDI for all developing countries increased by 28 points (from 0.26 to 0.54), which was substantially higher than that of India.

Thus, it is painful but true that India's performance in respect of socio-economic development in the previous three decades has been no better than performance on growth. On any indicator of socio-economic well-being—be it adult literacy, infant mortality, maternal mortality, life expectancy or gender bias—India's performance continues to be among the bottom one-third globally. What is worse is that progress in all these areas is much slower than other developing countries (leaving aside the least-developed countries).

At the time of Independence, for reasons which were entirely valid then, there was a strong intellectual conviction and political consensus in India that pro-poor policies and strategies had to be sharply distinguished from pro-growth and pro-trade policies. During the long period of colonial rule, India had a lot of trade combined with a lot of poverty, famine and disease. Unfortunately, despite the passage of time and phenomenal changes that have occurred in global economic relationships during the second half of the twentieth century, the haunted memories of our colonial past continues to shape the contours of the debate on economic policy. There is still a powerful and influential section in the political spectrum which considers pro-trade and pro-growth policies to be anti-poor.

There are multiple causes of persistent poverty in India. Despite the rhetoric, public expenditure policies have not favoured the expansion of social services for the poor. There are problems of governance, widespread administrative apathy and rampant corruption in the exercise of state power. Governments at the Centre, states and local levels are heavily debt ridden and virtually without means to care adequately for the poor. Nevertheless, the strong association between low growth and persistence of poverty in the last 50 years is too strong to ignore. Higher growth will not solve all problems, but given the necessary political will, it can definitely go a long way.

By 2025, chances are high of India's per capita income growing four times, provided the economy of India can sustain an annual growth rate of 8–9 per cent. Fresh jobs can be created at a rate much higher than the growth rate of the labour force, even when the employment elasticity is significantly less than unity. There is a greater chance of real wages increasing at a rate which is at least as high as per capita income, if not higher. As mentioned earlier, this has in fact been the experience of several fast-growing countries. Given the fact that the social and political environment are participatory in nature, there is no reason why the same should not happen in India. For the interest burden to be reduced in a significant manner, the government should reduce its public debt by reducing its debt-financed assets in the public sector. This will lead to a release of resources for greater investment in social sectors, particularly health and education. It is interesting to note that countries and regions which have succeeded in substantially raising their literacy rates are also those that have succeeded in alleviating poverty.

While ideal, it may be too optimistic a view. There is no doubt that post the recent favourable changes in the economic policy environment, an imminent need is to make substantial improvements in the overall policy framework, while at the same time enhance the efficiency with which resources are used. Considering the years of neglect, the physical infrastructure, especially the transport infrastructure is not in a good shape. Also, until there is a significant increase in the investment in energy, many parts of the country will face acute shortages of power. In respect of human resources, although India is at an advantageous situation due to the presence of a large network of institutions of technology and higher education, unfortunately, in recent years there has been a sharp decline in standards of training and education.

Therefore, before India can come to a point where it can exploit fresh opportunities in order to realize its full potential, there is a lot that must be done. However, the good news is that that these opportunities are here, and that the patterns of global trade and investment in the 1990s have changed in India's favour. The only binding constraint on India's economic future is the lack of a strong political will to move ahead decisively to overcome the shortcomings in the policies and administrative practices of the past. Hopefully a consensus will emerge, as a result of which India will be placed as one of the leading economies in the world in the twenty-first century.

Section 2

GOVERNANCE

5

THE PUBLIC SECTOR

In the twenty-first century, one of the most important economic issues before the country is the future role of the public sector. Unfortunately, the debate on this question has been highly ideological, with strong political overtones. A commitment to the expansion of the public sector is viewed as being synonymous with a commitment to the welfare of the poor. The public sector is also widely seen as an instrument for the promotion of social goals over private interests and as a symbol of national sovereignty.

As a means of distancing India from the colonial powers, these views had some merit at the time of Independence in 1947. Today, these are not only arcane but also damaging to national interest. A great deal of the present-day financial crisis can be attributed to the reckless expansion of the public sector at a substantial public cost.

Government Borrowings and Public Sector Losses

The central government alone has established many commercial enterprises, not counting the public financial institutions, insurance companies and railways. These include enterprises in construction, services and manufacturing. About half of the enterprises make losses, which have to be covered by fresh loans from the government or government banks. What this means is that the government has been accumulating additional public debt in order to meet both the capital and the revenue requirements of enterprises. The situation has become untenable as the government's debt has ballooned and revenue deficits have reached unprecedented proportions. A number of recent studies have highlighted the problem of India's internal debt. All reasonable projections of the government's debt position indicate that over time, interest payment by the government will exceed net new borrowings by it. In other words, the government will enter what is called the 'debt trap'. It will have to borrow more and more, at higher interest rates, to meet its interest obligations on old debt.

To a large extent, the fiscal crisis of the central government is a reflection of the financial crisis of the public sector. If investment in the public sector were more remunerative, or if the government had not borrowed to invest in public enterprises, the fiscal and the debt situation would have been much more manageable. Let us also consider the question: which section of the population suffers most because of the government's inability to keep its fiscal house in order? It is certainly not the affluent classes, who are likely to have actually benefited from fiscal expansion. The worst affected are likely to be the poor, the unemployed and the illiterate, who are dependent on public services, public investment and public programmes. For example, in India, where about half of the population is illiterate, *explicit* government subsidies to centrally owned public enterprises are more than five times the central government's budget for education. In other words, the elimination of explicit subsidies (not to speak of *implicit* subsidies, which are provided through preferential credit or pricing arrangements) could enable the government to substantially increase its outlay on education and other services for the poor.

The financial position of the state governments is even worse than that of the Centre. With a couple of exceptions, most states in India now have debts that they cannot repay, and revenue deficits that they cannot finance. Many states do not have the means to maintain their existing assets, provide adequate services to the people or undertake further investments, however urgent or crucial. An important reason for the state of 'fiscal incapacity' is, without doubt, the failure of public-sector enterprises to generate adequate revenue or return on past investments.

Why did these 'temples of modern India,' as Pandit Jawaharlal Nehru once called them, fail so miserably in strengthening India's industrial and economic outlook? There was a time, soon after Independence, when the public sector was considered as the principal instrument for raising the level of savings and growth in the economy. At the time, investment rates in the economy were low (about 10 per cent in 1950–51), and the private sector did not have the financial means or technological capacity to undertake large, new investments in industry and infrastructure. The government, therefore, had to take upon itself the task of mobilizing the necessary financial and technical resources and setting up new industries in the public sector. It was expected that as these industries came into production and profits were made, these profits would be further reinvested in the public sector. Thus, savings and investment rates would rise, and growth rates would be accelerated. Since the production pattern in the economy would also reflect social priorities, the objectives of both growth and equity would be achieved.

The government did succeed in mobilizing substantial resources through taxes and borrowings and pumping them into the public sector. A number of large enterprises, on a scale hitherto unknown in India, were set up in the 1950s and 1960s. These opened up many parts of the country which had seen no industrial activity in the past. India also became a sizeable producer of machinery, steel and heavy equipment in which the industrial world had a virtual monopoly. In these and other ways, the public sector began to symbolize the hopes and aspirations of a nation that had become free after a long and protracted political struggle.

The public sector expanded rapidly. By 1988–89, it accounted for more than half the domestic output (at factor cost) in mining, manufacturing, electricity, construction, banking and insurance. However, while physical output and financial investments were expanding, productivity and profitability of the public sector were declining for a variety of reasons. The government—at the Centre and in the states—became heavily involved not only in planning and guiding investment priorities, but in actually managing enterprises. Since most public-sector enterprises operated as monopolies, without internal or external competition, there was no financial accountability or pressure to generate profits. The government became the sole source of funds for investment and the sole arbiter of how public-sector resources were to be used. The sector also became, over time, the principal source of providing fully secure jobs at wages that were rising faster than elsewhere in the economy. A multiplicity of trade unions, owing allegiance to different political parties, emerged in different plants. This had the effect of further politicizing the public sector, and placing a discount on productive efficiency.

As the sector became more politicized and more politically controlled, it also became financially unviable. Over time, it acquired multiple roles—as a provider of jobs, saviour of sick enterprises, supplier of social services and a source of funds. In this situation, the spread of political and administrative corruption was unavoidable. There were contracts to be awarded, technologies to be selected, supplies to be procured, services to be bought and managers to be appointed. The government, through its ministers and administrators, began intervening in all these decisions. Inevitably, political and personal considerations became dominant factors in decision-making. While all this was going on in public-sector factories and plants, the government also became financially weak. It started to rely more and more on borrowings, rather than its own savings, for financing public investments.

Experience of Some Developing Countries

This situation could be halfway tolerable if public enterprises were functioning effectively in physical terms, and commercial losses were due to subsidies for the poor. But this was not the case. Most of these enterprises operated at levels of physical efficiency which were lower than similar enterprises in developed as well as developing countries. Research on the efficiency of power undertakings in developing countries shows that:

i. The Indian power industry, on an average, is only half as efficient as that of China. The worst performers are Uttar Pradesh (UP), Odisha, Punjab, Haryana and Bihar. Their efficiency index is *one-third* that of China.
ii. India's transmission losses alone are three times that of China. A reduction in such losses to reasonable levels could lead to additional revenues of at least ₹4,000 crore per year even at low tariff levels (and more than ₹6,000 crore at higher tariff levels).
iii. China's average costs of supplying electricity are 78 per cent of its tariffs. This yields substantial operational surplus which is reinvested in further electricity generation. If India's cost to tariff ratio were the same as that of China, it could generate additional revenue of ₹12,500 crore per year.

iv. As is well known, there is substantial excess labour in the state electricity boards. However, the interesting point to note is that additional revenue of ₹17,000–₹18,000 crore per year is possible without firing even a single employee if transmission losses and cost–tariff ratios could be brought to the Chinese levels. In fact, if this amount of internal resources were available, India could generate at least half a million additional jobs per year in power and related industries.

The last point is of great significance in considering the policy options for the reform of the public sector. The perpetuation of loss-making and inefficient public enterprises is generally projected as being in the interest of labour or the poor. This is far from the truth. The reform of the public sector, including the closure of unproductive and persistently loss-making or sick enterprises, can be brought about without hurting labour or the poor. In fact, such reform can be a major source of revenue and generation of new employment opportunities for the poor.

It is, of course, true that the reform process can be mismanaged or the economic situation can be allowed to deteriorate to a point where the reform of public enterprises is not possible without massive unemployment or the loss of incomes for the poor. Such a situation can be avoided if the reform programme is transparent and is adopted at an early stage after consultations with labour. The evidence is overwhelming that workers and the poor are likely to be much better off in an economy where the revenue position of the government is strong, and where investments are increasing rather than decreasing. As far as the poor are concerned, the ideological debate about 'public vs private' is simply irrelevant in today's democratic and socially conscious political environment. What the poor need are jobs and resources, not a loss-making public sector.

The Question of Privatization

In the last five years, there has been a phenomenal change in the attitude of developing countries towards the privatization of public-sector enterprises. In the early 1980s, when 'privatization' was first introduced in the United Kingdom (UK), there was considerable scepticism about the efficacy of this policy. Later, in the second half of the 1980s, several debt-ridden countries in Latin America and Africa were compelled to adopt privatization as a means of solving their debt problems through the use of instruments such as debt-equity swaps. Currently, with a few exceptions, almost all developing countries have declared themselves in favour of privatization. This shift in views is partly a result of the collapse of the command economy structures in several parts of the world. The aggressive drive towards privatization in Eastern Europe and the former Soviet Union has constituted a powerful example. Partly, the shift in policy reflects the failure of most developing countries to find alternative viable solutions to the problems of their public enterprises.

There seems to have been a similar shift in the academic opinion on the importance of ownership, whether it should be public or private, in determining industrial performance. Earlier, based primarily on the experience of privatized industries in the UK and some Latin American countries, several studies had concluded that a competitive environment, rather than ownership, seemed to be the key to efficiency. Further, it was argued that the policy environment within which public enterprises operated, as well as their management structure, had more to do with their performance, relative to private enterprises, than having the ownership of their assets. Research, however, seems to suggest that ownership per se is an important factor in determining the performance of enterprises. By and large, privately owned firms have a tendency to perform better than publicly owned firms under similar market structures. Another conclusion is that, in most firms, both consumer satisfaction as well as workers' welfare seem to have improved after privatization. The gains came primarily from improved productivity, increased investment and better pricing. Incremental gains occurred in both competitive and monopoly markets, in part because of a regulatory framework that protected consumers. The gains were shared by all the parties involved, including the government, workers and consumers.

The theoretical and practical case for privatization is based on the following arguments:

i. Private ownership establishes a market for managers, which improves the quality of management.
ii. Private firms are subject to capital market disciplines and scrutiny by financial experts. The ability to

raise funds for growth is crucially dependent on performance. On the other hand, government ownership and budget support can provide easy access to credit for public enterprises irrespective of their performance.

iii. Private firms are more subject to liquidation, threat of takeovers and loss of assets for owners than public corporations. When owners stand to lose control over assets, there is a greater likelihood of remedial measures being taken.

iv. Political interference is unavoidable in public corporations and is a major cause of the decline in operational efficiency. Such political decision-making reflects itself in the less than optimal choice of technology or location, overstaffing, inefficient use of inputs and purchase or price preferences for certain suppliers. Most governments also impose non-economic objectives on public corporations.

v. The boards of private corporations, where ownership is widely dispersed, are more accountable than tightly controlled or publicly owned corporations. Bureaucrats on the boards of public corporations are generally insensitive to efficiency considerations.

vi. Efforts to improve managerial efficiency in public enterprises by administrative measures are generally short-lived and unsustainable as, sooner or later, political considerations take precedence over economic or commercial considerations.

Despite the benefits of privatization, it will be a mistake to regard it as a panacea for all the ills of the public sector. In some countries, where privatization has been carefully planned and where the economy as a whole is functioning efficiently, it has indeed improved industrial performance. In several other countries, however, privatization has not yielded positive results for the economy as a whole (as in some of the countries of the former Soviet Union). In some other countries, because of implementation problems, the privatization process had to be slowed down or halted. The only general conclusion that can be derived from this varied experience is that the success or otherwise of the policy of privatization is likely to depend on the country's circumstances, particularly its macroeconomic performance. If macroeconomic policies are good and the economy is growing, privatization is likely to succeed. Otherwise, hasty privatization may give rise to higher unemployment and a worsening of the poverty situation.

India is one of the few countries where there is, as yet, no consensus in favour of the privatization of all public enterprises. If anything, public opinion is generally against privatization as a policy tool. On the whole, however, there is a strong case to take a more positive view of privatization of financially weak public enterprises. This case is not based on any presumed inherent superiority of private enterprises over public enterprises. Nor is it based on any ideological grounds. The case for privatization is twofold. First and foremost, it is to enable the government (as the owner) to reduce its liabilities to the public. The sale of unproductive assets is the only feasible means to avert a domestic debt crisis.

A second reason is the inability of the central and state governments to find an effective alternative solution to problems of the public sector. The need to introduce an 'arm's length' relationship between the government and the public sector has been on the policy agenda for several decades, but, in actual practice, not much has changed. Public enterprises continue to suffer from day-to-day formal and informal interventions by the government; top-management positions continue to remain vacant and the sector continues to be a drain on the national and state budgets. Electoral compulsions and extraneous considerations continue to be the guiding factors in investment and production decisions, and the public sector continues to provide a relatively autonomous mechanism for the exercise of political patronage and power. Recently, some policy initiatives have been taken to make the sector more accountable, but results so far have not been satisfactory.

Public-Sector Reforms in India

In recent years, there have been four positive developments concerning the reform of the public sector in India. First, and perhaps the most significant for the future, is the partial disinvestment of equity of selected enterprises. In many cases, the extent of disinvestment is still small. Nonetheless, it is an important step in the commercialization of enterprises and in making them subject to open public scrutiny. Second, public-sector enterprises, including banks, are being encouraged to raise fresh equity directly from the public rather than from the government. If carried to its logical conclusion, the expansion of enterprises depends on their ability to attract capital from the public which, in turn, depends on their financial performance. Third, public-sector monopolies are subject to competition from new private enterprises in most sectors. A competitive environment is a necessary, though not a sufficient, condition for the efficient use of resources by enterprises. Fourth, steps have been taken to make the institutional relationship between the government and commercial enterprises more contractual, and less ad hoc. A formal and contractual relationship is more conducive to better performance than an informal and ad hoc system of supervision and control.

However, these measures are not sufficient to impart dynamism to the economy or to restore the fiscal balance. India's internal debt is becoming unmanageable, and it is no longer feasible to provide revenue or capital support to public enterprises. In fact, in the next few years, fiscal prudence as well as the welfare objectives for the poor, require that the burden of interest payments on this debt is drastically reduced. A reduction in public debt is likely if part of the public-sector assets is sold to the public and receipts are used to retire public debt (which, in any case, is partly incurred to create these assets).

This combination, of the partial sale of equity in well-performing enterprises and outright sale of sick enterprises, can generate substantial resources (despite some temporary problems due to volatility of the domestic capital market). As experience shows, shares of profit-making enterprises, including banks, can be sold at a substantial premium over book value. The sale of loss-making enterprises, in addition to recouping some past investments, also relieves the budget from the burden of financing losses of such enterprises. This policy should be implemented over a period of time after sufficient notice so that the entire process is open and transparent. Sufficient worldwide experience is now available to ensure that a partial or outright sale of public enterprises can be accomplished without hurting the interests of consumers, workers or the government.

A legitimate question that may be asked is: if the disinvestment policy is so sound, why is there no political consensus in India in favour of it? If outright sales of public enterprises can be achieved without hurting the interests of workers, and also result in substantial economic benefit for the country, then why do trade unions and others continue to oppose the privatization of even sick enterprises? The answer to these questions can be found in the context in which this issue has been debated in India. The ills of public enterprises have generally been attributed to problems of 'overstaffing' or high labour costs. As a result, a proposal to sell an enterprise or reduce government shareholding is seen as a first step in the process of closing an enterprise and loss of livelihood for workers. Many public enterprises in India are indeed overstaffed, but this is not the most important cause of operational inefficiency or budgetary drain. In several sectors, it is possible to achieve substantial savings in costs and efficiency without declaring a single redundancy and without reducing the wage rate. In other cases, workers' interests can be protected either by guaranteeing continued employment or by providing full compensation for any potential loss of wages.

A further difficulty in disinvestment is that public-sector losses ultimately constitute a private benefit for some section of the society, or for some specific person. The cost of these losses to society as a whole is not apparent to the public, and in any case, does not adversely affect policymakers. In order to increase public awareness of costs and benefits, it may be desirable to use part of receipts from the sale of enterprises to finance a perceived public benefit. For example, the financing of food (or fertilizer) subsidies could, over a period of time, be shifted from the budget to a separate fund for social (or agricultural) development. A part of the receipts from the sale of enterprises could be credited to such a fund.

In order to gain public credibility, it is also important to ensure that the disinvestment process is fair and transparent and that public perceptions of political interference and favouritism are avoided. Surveys of privatization experience show that different approaches to disinvestment bring different results. The following are some of the lessons from cases of successful disinvestment in different countries. These can provide useful and practical guidelines for India:

i. Gains from disinvestment are usually higher when the transaction is transparent, competitive and fair and is undertaken as part of a wider programme of reforms to make the economy more competitive.

ii. Once the ground rules for disinvestment are well established, many potentially competitive firms can be divested without complex regulation. Breaking up firms to reduce their market power can enhance competition. If the public enterprise is a natural monopoly, a well-designed regulatory framework, setting forth the obligations of the government and the buyer, is critical to positive results.
iii. Although the government sometimes may have to absorb part of the debt in order to make a firm attractive to potential buyers, more extensive investments in restructuring do not usually pay off in terms of higher privatization proceeds.
iv. With a strong independent agency in place to oversee disinvestments, actual implementation can be decentralized.
v. Competitive bidding is preferable to a negotiated sale. Competitive bidding not only improves the sale price but also creates pressures for a more transparent process because competing bidders insist on clear rules.
vi. Prequalifying bidders and requiring buyers to put up sufficient equity are important in preventing later defaults, but restrictions on the types of bidders or on the resale of parts of the firms by new owners reduce the sale price and competitiveness of the bidding process.

Another important priority for the future is to reduce the managerial role of the government in enterprises where it is likely to continue to have a majority shareholding (e.g. enterprises that are yielding adequate returns on capital). The government should also completely relinquish the powers to appoint CEOs or senior managers of a corporation. In the past, several enterprises have suffered because of the government's inability to make such appointments in time. There are many public-sector units without managing directors, some for as long as 10 years. This is a sorry state of affairs. Such appointments are also subject to political pulls and pressures, which are likely to increase with different parties forming governments, individually or in coalition, at the central and state level. In the future, such appointments should be made by the boards of the corporations. The boards, in turn, should be elected by all shareholders, including the government, on the basis of managerial competence in an open general meeting. If necessary, a body similar to the UPSC may be appointed to advise on board appointments.

A decision has been taken by the government to permit private investment in sectors that were earlier reserved for the public sector. As a matter of policy, all public-sector enterprises which dominate the market in any product (with, say, more than 50 per cent of the market share) should be broken up, and one or more of the component pieces should be sold to the public. While ownership is important, a competitive environment matters in determining the relative performance of enterprises (whether private or public). A competitive environment also promotes allocative efficiency, encourages innovation and lowers prices for the consumers.

Such an environment, contrary to popular perceptions, is also better for workers as it is conducive to greater labour mobility.

Governments in all countries are called upon to provide a number of public services to the community, such as education, healthcare, electricity, telecommunications, urban transport, water and sewerage. It is also the conventional wisdom that only the public sector can supply public services, particularly in developing countries, where the bulk of beneficiaries are economically backward and do not have the capacity to pay. As a result, many developing countries, including India, have set up elaborate public-sector mechanisms to supply public services. Unfortunately, the actual delivery of public services is abysmally inadequate because of the scarcity of resources, poor maintenance, untrained and unresponsive staff, poor accountability, and widespread corruption. Paradoxically, the poor have little or no effective access to these services and have to rely on the private sector for their necessities. The actual supply of public-sector services is generally confined to the better-off sections of the society. Thus, for example, it is not uncommon for the very poor in several countries to depend on private vendors for the supply of water, while homeowners are supplied with free piped water by public authorities.

There is no easy solution to this problem. However, it is becoming increasingly evident that standards of public services can be improved dramatically if greater use is made of non-governmental organizations (NGOs), private corporations and individuals for the supply of these services. This can be done either through contracting out certain services or by granting franchises. A successful example of this practice in India is the franchise granted by telecommunication authorities to private individuals and shops for establishing public call offices for long-distance telephone calls. In several cities, the acute shortage of public phones has been virtually eliminated with considerable benefit for the common person. This practice has also generated substantial additional employment.

It should be emphasized that the provision of public services through non-governmental sources does not necessarily imply that the full cost of providing such services must be recovered from the users. It is open to the government to provide subsidies for the provision of specific services, say primary education or water to the poor, if it so wishes. The crucial question is not whether the governments should participate in the provision of services or whether these services should be subsidized, but what form such participation or subsidy should take. The government should thus put in place standards of service, monitor performance and ensure access to the poor. However, it does not necessarily have to get directly involved in delivering all essential public services.

To conclude, a reduction in the role of the public sector in the economy is now essential. This is not a question of ideology or the presumed superiority of one type of economic system over another. This is a matter of practical necessity in view of the unsustainability of the public-debt profile in India. It is also in the interest of equity. The poor are likely to be better served if some of the resources currently being employed to support public-sector enterprises are released for financing social sectors, including anti-poverty programmes.

6

GOODS AND SERVICES

The focus of attention in conventional economics, including development economics, was on the production of goods—manufactured products and agricultural commodities. It was, of course, recognized that the services sector (which includes transport, communication, trade, banking, construction, public administration, etc.) was an important source of income and employment in most economies. However, overall, the growth of services was perceived at best as a by-product of developments in the primary and secondary sectors, and at worst as a drag on the prospects for long-term economic growth. Services were believed to be mainly non-tradable activities with slow productivity growth and low employment potential.

The Services Revolution

In recent years, there has been a phenomenal change in the conventional view of services and their role in the economy (although, in India, the conventional view still dominates the public debate). The development of certain services is crucial for economic growth. Services of various kinds are getting delinked from the manufacturing process and are becoming essential elements of the productive structure. In addition to the manufacture of the many industrial products, they are also being designed, marketed, advertised, distributed, leased and serviced. A significant and rising part of the value added by manufacturers now consists of services.

The massive growth in the technologies of computer and communication is ultimately the result of a change in the role and image of services. One can clearly see that the levels of industrialization, along with geography are not the key aspects deciding the facilities for the production of services. From being mere recipients to important providers of long-distance services, developing countries are coming out of the shadow of playing traditional roles. India has also participated in the export of certain services (e.g. software) which is expanding faster than the overall trade. The potential for expansion of jobs and incomes in the services sector is truly immense. From India's point of view, some of the recent global developments, which provide opportunities for substantial growth, are the following:

i. Progress in IT is making it increasingly possible to unbundle the production and consumption of information-intensive service activities. These activities—R&D, computing, inventory management, quality control, accounting, personnel administration, secretarial, marketing, advertising, distribution and legal services—are performed in all economic sectors. They play a fundamental role not only in the service industries but also in manufacturing and primary industries. The feasibility of these activities has become more prominent with the progress made in IT.

ii. With the growth in technological innovation, the opportunities for services to be embodied in goods that are traded internationally are expanding by leaps and bounds. Therefore, if India were to become an efficient supplier of services, it should not allow itself to become a low-cost producer of certain types of goods (e.g. computers or discs).

iii. Compared with prices in other services, the global prices of services like transport and communication saw a dramatic fall. Sea transport costs were less than a third of their 1920 level by 1960, and this phenomenon has been continuing so. In addition to this, networks are becoming more and more global, while the cost of communication is also becoming independent of distance. The foremost example is that of the Internet, which links millions of computers around the world. With its advent, several large corporations have been able to successfully build networks to meet their global communication needs.

India's geographical distance from several important industrial markets is no longer an important element in the cost structure of skills-based services.

iv. The pattern of demand in industrial countries in favour of services is witnessing a structural shift, along with incomes and employment. There is a decline in the share of the manufacturing sector of rich countries, which means that there is a relative decline in their demand for industrial raw materials and fuels. It in turn means that the growth in exports of developing countries is dependant more on efficiency in providing services and service-intensive goods, and less on natural resource endowments.

In view of these developments in production and trade in products and services, it is clear that the expansion of high technology and knowledge-based services have an important place in any strategy for the rapid growth of incomes and jobs in India in the twenty-first century. Although India has done well in exports of software and certain other value-added services, the progress in creating a supportive physical and human infrastructure has been relatively slow. In physical infrastructure, a competitive telecommunication system is especially important to the development of long-distance services. Recent technological advances in telecommunications have made it possible to create an efficient low-cost and high-volume system within a short period of three–four years. India must move decisively on this front. In respect of human infrastructure, India has the advantage of a large network of institutions of technology and higher education. The drawback is that except for a few institutions, there has been a sharp decline in standards of training and education. It is necessary to reinvigorate the institutional infrastructure by making it more performance-oriented, market-sensitive and self-supporting. On a wider front, the diffusion of computer literacy must receive special attention in the country's educational strategy at secondary and higher levels.

The domestic regulatory environment also needs to be completely overhauled in order to capture the opportunities offered by the internationalization of services. Liberalizing the import and investment regimes is central. There should be no quota restrictions or duties (assuming a competitive exchange rate) on imports or exports of knowledge-based services. Similarly, foreign investment in this sector should be permitted without any limits or restrictions, as foreign direct investment is a major vehicle for the international delivery of services and dissemination of technical knowledge.

Government policy should make special efforts to foster a domestic competitive environment with no barriers to entry. Existing state or private monopolies need to be broken, as competition would provide the greatest assurance for technology to be continuously updated and for costs to remain internationally competitive. Given forward-looking policies and strong governmental support, there is little doubt that India can emerge as a leading global supplier of knowledge-based information services. Exports of such services can generate new jobs faster than manufacturing and provide an effective answer to the problem of the educated unemployed in the twenty-first century.

Revitalization of Industry

The priority to be accorded to the development of new services should not imply any neglect of the commodity-producing sectors—either in industry or in agriculture. If an overall growth rate of 7–8 per cent in national income is achieved, India has to do a lot better than in the past, in respect of industry as well as agriculture. Despite the close attention given to industrial development, the growth record is unsatisfactory and well below announced targets. Leaving aside the 1990s, when growth rates dipped significantly because of the economic crisis, the manufacturing sector (including the unregistered sector) grew at an annual rate of just 5 per cent over a period of 40 years since 1950. It is interesting to note that the performance was quite satisfactory during the early years of 1950–60 as well as during the 1980s, when growth rates were close to a respectable 8 per cent per annum. The worst period was between 1966 and 1980, when the growth rate was only 3.5 per cent per annum. It is no coincidence that this was also the period when industrial policies became overtly 'social' and highly interventionist. To achieve the so-called social objectives, additional controls and regulations were overlaid on the already-overburdened industrial and trade control system and tariff protection became progressively higher.

The Indian industrial policies, and their effect on India's development, have been a subject of intense academic research and considerable public debate, both domestically and internationally. After all, India was the first developing country to consciously adopt a development strategy that sought to break the historical (and colonial) patterns of trade and production through democratic means. The strategy was supported by a strong national consensus, as it constituted a reasonable approach to overcome colonial deprivation and neglect. It was also consistent with the economic thought that was then internationally dominant. Nevertheless, while politically inspiring, this strategy failed to yield the expected economic results.

India continued to engage in micro-level domestic industrial planning even after it became evident that there was a clear mismatch between the announced priorities and macroeconomic policies to support these priorities. Thus, for example, India gave the highest priority to the production of capital goods. Tariff policies, on the other hand, gave them negative protection. Labour-using industries such as the engineering industry were discriminated against, whereas capital-using and high-cost industries such as petrochemicals received fiscal encouragement. While in several other developing countries, the government's intervention was positive and gave competitive inducements to efficiency, in India such intervention became negative and encouraged monopolistic production.

There is no unanimity among experts on the macroeconomic determinants of and constraints on industrial growth in India. There are alternative hypotheses about factors underlying industrial stagnation between 1965 and 1980, and the resurgence of industrial growth since the 1980s. In the latter period, there was some liberalization of industrial and trade policies, and fiscal policies were more expansionary. However, the overall framework of macroeconomic policies remained interventionist. The historical picture is further complicated by the fact that during the period from 1965 to 1980, India suffered from several droughts, two external oil shocks (in 1974 and 1979, respectively) and a war with Pakistan. It is difficult to quantify and isolate the impact of these factors on industrial growth from the effect of macroeconomic policies.

Nevertheless, the fact remains that, as compared with the period 1965–80, there was a sharp increase in total factor productivity and efficiency of industrial investment since 1981. There was also a significant increase in the rate of investment in the economy (the rate of gross fixed capital formation in the economy increased from an average of about 16 per cent of gross national product [GNP] in the earlier period to nearly 22 per cent in the 1980s). This improvement in productivity of investment could not have occurred without a significant improvement in the investment climate. The liberalization of industrial and trade policies during this period, modest as it was, must have played a role in bringing about this favourable outcome. Relatively small relaxations in industrial controls, and a more pragmatic import policy, seem to have resulted in a large increase in capacity utilization and efficiency. Much of this improvement was reflected in a substantial increase in the real rates of return on investment in the private manufacturing sector. There was some improvement in the efficiency of public-sector manufacturing investment also, but in absolute terms, such investment remained highly unproductive.

Another finding of research is that in the 1960s and 1970s, there was considerable repression of industrial demand through restrictive licencing of production of consumer goods and increases in indirect taxes. This led to a recession in the capital and intermediate goods sectors. The low domestic output of consumer goods could not support the capacity created for the production of capital and intermediate goods. Unfortunately, much of this capacity was too inefficient to be competitive in export markets. After the 1980s, on the other hand, the liberalization of industrial licencing policy helped the growth of the consumer goods sector, which, in turn, increased demand and capacity utilization in the intermediate and capital goods sector. Indirect taxes as a proportion of selling prices of manufactured goods remained stable on the whole and did not choke off demand. The increase in factor productivity helped make India's exports more competitive. Exports were also helped by a more realistic exchange rate policy, particularly after the second half of the 1980s. Growth in exports had a positive link with growth in output.

There are important lessons for the future in this story. It is clear that repression of consumer demand, through high taxes or production restrictions, is not in the interest of industrial growth and employment. Investment and growth in the intermediate and capital goods sector are dependent on the growth of the final demand. A competitive environment for exports is also critical, not only for the balance of payments but also for growth of output. Rising domestic demand can be translated into growth in output only if markets are competitive, and firms are motivated to make their profits from volumes rather than prices. High rates of protection are not conducive to efficiency or growth in domestic output. In the initial stages of industrialization, protection can help domestic firms by displacing imports; however, after some time, excessive protection from imports tends to raise prices rather than output. Finally, there is strong evidence that the contribution of the public sector to the growth of manufacturing output since the mid-1960s has been negative, or at best marginal. The public sector has pre-empted a large part of the society's savings without making an equivalent contribution to the growth of output or investment. The public sector's contribution to infrastructure development has been more positive. Public investment in infrastructure provided a supportive environment for the growth of industrial output.

Some of these lessons have been reflected in the industrial policy changes introduced after 1991. The most negative features of the old policy have been modified or eliminated. Industrial licencing has been abolished from most sectors of the economy, effective rates of protection have been reduced gradually, foreign direct investment is being encouraged, exchange controls have been liberalized, capital issue control has been removed, the tax regime has been simplified and government intervention has become much more positive.

Despite several amendments over the years, the basic legislative framework for the regulation of companies and corporations, under the Company Law, is pre-War in origin. This framework cannot adequately reflect the modern-day realities of corporate behaviour and international commerce, which is characterized by the fast and periodic restructuring of management, shifts in product mix, and acquisitions and mergers in response to changing technologies and demand. Indian corporate legislation needs to adapt to these changes and minimize the involvement of the government in the enforcement of legislation. Independent regulatory and quasi-judicial bodies should be set up where necessary. Judicial processes should be simplified to make it possible to enforce commercial contracts and to promote responsible corporate behaviour.

Macroeconomic policies—particularly fiscal, financial and tariff policies—have important effects on industrial behaviour. In this century, these policies have become more growth oriented and less inward looking. The process of policy reform needs to be further strengthened. Exports should be supported through a further reduction of tariffs and equalization of effective protection rates across sectors. The exclusive concern of industrial regulatory policies should be to encourage competitiveness and transparency in corporate behaviour. Rules for disclosure of public information have to be comprehensive and need to be strictly enforced. Fiscal policy should be neutral between different types of industrial activity and technological choices. It is also important for fiscal policy to be stable and predictable.

India has the industrial and entrepreneurial base to break away decisively from the industrial stagnation of the earlier decades. The recent changes in IT, trade patterns and structure of capital flows are also favourable to India. A sustained industrial growth rate of 8–10 per cent per annum is achievable and must be the goal of India's economic policy in the future.

Investment in Agriculture

As in the case of industry, the post-Independence development strategy also called for widespread state intervention in all aspects of the production and distribution of agricultural commodities. It is interesting to note that most of the instruments of intervention and legislation affecting agriculture were devised to meet scarcity situations associated with famines and the Second World War. Despite important changes in India's agricultural situation, the pre-War legislative framework has survived. As agriculture is a state subject, the extent and the variety of instruments used to intervene in the agricultural sector also vary from state to state. Among examples of controls and regulation affecting agriculture are the following:

i. There are licencing requirements for wholesale trade, storage and processing of virtually all agricultural commodities in all states.

ii. Official permits are required for out-of-state sales of some commodities; and

iii. There have been limits on the storage of agricultural products, such as rice (in Maharashtra, Punjab and Andhra Pradesh), wheat (in West Bengal and Madhya Pradesh), sugar (in Kerala), and virtually all food commodities in UP and Tamil Nadu.

Apart from the fact that several of the above mechanisms to regulate agriculture are no longer relevant, there is also considerable instability in the regulatory regime. Often, various kinds of limits or restrictions are changed in the marketing season on the basis of inadequate or misleading information. There is an urgent need to dispense with most of the petty controls and establish a stable and relatively free regulatory regime for the production and movement of goods. There should be a thorough review of the entire legislative framework in light of modern realities, and the absence of famines and scarcities of the type prevalent earlier. A drastic simplification of the regulatory regime can result in considerable cost savings in agricultural administration, in addition to improving returns to farmers.

Agricultural growth is not only vital for the economy but also central to the welfare of the bulk of India's population. Agriculture accounts for almost 65 per cent of employment in the country and nearly 300 million of the poor live and work in rural areas. Unfortunately, the proportion of the population in agriculture has remained practically static since Independence. Agricultural growth rates have been even lower than the low growth rate of the economy as a whole. As a result, the disparity between per capita incomes in agriculture and other sectors has been accentuated over the years. The employment elasticity of growth in the manufacturing and other sectors of the economy has been relatively small, and what is worse, growth rates in other sectors have not been high enough to pull labour out of agriculture. Herein lies the importance of accelerating growth rates in the national economy as a means of reducing the incidence of poverty.

Irrigation and new technology were the two most important sources of growth in agriculture after the mid-1960s. After Independence, India invested heavily in major and minor irrigation schemes to reduce its dependence on uncertain monsoons. India created one of the largest agricultural research and education systems in the world, with a massive infrastructure consisting of a network of central institutes, state universities and zonal research stations. The success of the Green Revolution in increasing agricultural yields was in no small measure due to the work of these research institutions. Unfortunately, in both these crucial areas—irrigation and research—severe problems have emerged in recent years.

Since most of the easier and cost-effective options for expanding the irrigation potential have been utilized, the real hectare costs of major irrigation schemes have increased sharply. At the same time, public and private investment in agriculture in general, and irrigation in particular, has declined. The decline in public investment in agriculture, which is an important source of investment in public irrigation schemes, has been sharper than that in private investment. This has hurt the poor farmer in addition to curbing the potential for growth in irrigation.

The lack of adequate financial resources and efficient planning has affected the timely completion of ongoing projects. Delays of several years in completing major and medium irrigation schemes are common. In all states, there is a tendency to start new projects even though ongoing projects are under-funded. The actual returns to irrigation investment have been further reduced by insufficient allocation of funds for the operation and maintenance of completed projects. Operational budgets are generally a fraction of recommended norms, and expenditure is heavily skewed towards wages and salaries (which account for 95 per cent of budgets in some states). As a result, non-wage components of maintenance expenditure have shrunk, and signs of poor maintenance—silt deposits, broken linings and damaged structures—are visible in most surface irrigation schemes. Similarly, pumping equipment in many public tube wells generally remains out of order.

Similar problems of inadequate funding and poor maintenance are now emerging in agricultural research. These constitute a serious threat to the development of new technologies. After the Green Revolution, there have been no major breakthroughs in agricultural technologies in India, particularly in respect of 'rainfed' areas. Rainfed agriculture accounts for a major proportion of agricultural output, including over 60 per cent of rice, and most coarse grains, pulses, oilseeds and cotton. The availability of improved varieties of seeds for these areas remains limited, in part due to the concentration on the development of irrigated wheat and rice varieties, and in part due to differences in agro-climatic conditions in different regions of the country. As the area available for further expansion of the irrigation system becomes more limited, a sustained increase in agricultural productivity will increasingly depend on rainfed agriculture. There is usually a gestation period of 10–15 years before newly developed technologies can become fully operational. As such, there is an urgent need for a strong research effort in respect of rainfed and other problem areas relating to soil use.

There is a growing perception among agricultural scientists in India as well as government committees examining the issue that the agricultural research system is not responding well to the present-day needs of the agricultural economy. Research is generally too narrowly focussed and its quality seems to have declined in recent years. There is an inadequate focus on regional issues and a lack of effective monitoring of its results. Research activity also suffers from inadequate funding, suboptimal resource use and erosion in the quality of researchers. There are too many institutions with very little coordination among them on the content and priorities of research.

In addition to measures to improve the efficiency of resource use in irrigation and research, there is also a need to increase budgetary allocations for investment in irrigation and research. It is not as if the central and state governments have been neglecting agriculture in their expenditure plans.

Aggregate public expenditure has shot up sharply over the years, but the bulk of it has gone into the current expenditure in the form of an increased level of subsidies for fertilizer, irrigation, electricity, credit and other agricultural inputs rather than investment. In addition to the direct budgetary cost of 'explicit' subsidies, there is also the much larger flow of 'implicit' subsidies because of unrecovered costs in a whole range of agricultural services.

In view of the high fiscal deficit at the Centre and in the states, there is very little scope for increasing public investment in agriculture unless there is a shift in the composition of expenditure from the current to the capital account. Without growth in public investment, growth in private investment is also not feasible, as the two sources of investment in agriculture are generally complementary.

Acceleration in the rate of investment in agriculture is an important challenge for public policy in the next few years. Without it, sustained growth in the agricultural sector will not occur. There are, of course, a host of other important issues pertaining to agriculture that require attention. These include the removal of inter-crop imbalance, reorganization of agricultural credit, liberalizing agricultural exports and revitalizing extension, among others. However, corrective action in all these areas will become easier if sufficient resources are available to increase investment in agriculture and related sectors.

The opportunities for growth in new services, industry and agriculture are truly immense. If these opportunities are seized, India's national income can grow by 7–8 per cent per annum. If sustained over a period of two decades, growth rates of this order can make a major dent in the problem of poverty in India. This is precisely what happened in East Asia during the 30-year period from 1970–2000. There is no fundamental reason why this cannot happen in India.

7

FINANCE AND DEVELOPMENT: WHICH WAY NOW?

After the liberalization of the economy in 1991, there has been a fundamental change in the role of the financial system in India's economy. Part of this change is due to the changing role being assigned to the government and the public sector in the allocation of the nation's savings for development. A more dramatic reason for this change is the Asian Financial Crisis of the late 1990s. This crisis, and its aftermath, have brought to the fore the critical role of the financial system in determining the stability and sustainability of the real economy. As a result, the reform of the financial system, and the rules and the codes that should govern the conduct of financial business, figure high on the domestic agenda for reform as well as the international agenda for global cooperation.

Finance and Development: The Shifting Paradigm

As we reflect on the history of human civilization, it is surprising to recall just how recent the story of economic growth is. As American economist Paul Krugman noted:

> Economic growth, at least economic growth that raises living standards, is a modern invention. From the dawn of history to the eighteenth century, the world was essentially Malthusian. Improvements in technology and capital investments were always overtaken by population growth; the number of people slowly increased, but their average standards of living did not.[3]

Till the end of the nineteenth century, the only countries where per capita incomes were increasing on a sustained basis for any length of time were the ones in the West, particularly, England, Germany, France and the United States (US). During this entire period, the then so-called underdeveloped or Third World countries continued to be exporters of primary products and importers of industrial products with stagnant, and in some cases, declining per capita incomes. A large number of them were also colonies of the western powers, and the connection between these two situations—the colonial state and income stagnation—was not missed by their leaders and intellectuals.

The development strategies of the newly independent and developing countries in the mid-nineteenth century

---

[3]Krugman, Paul, *The Return of Depression Economics*, Penguin Press, London, 1999.

were framed against this background. The central and the leading role for breaking away from the colonial legacy and for speeding up the process of industrialization was assigned to the State. The need for the government to occupy the commanding heights and to lead from the top received further support from the astounding success of the Soviet Union in emerging as a rival centre of political and industrial power within a very short period. India, at that time, played a pioneering role in giving expression to the aspirations of the newly independent Third World countries in the economic field. Thus, in 1956, India's Second Five-Year Plan outlined the goals of development strategy in the following terms:

> The pattern of development and the structure of socio-economic relations should be so planned that they result not only in appreciable increases in national income and employment but also in greater equality in incomes and wealth. Major decisions regarding production, distribution, consumption and investment—and in fact all significant socio-economic relationships—must be made by agencies informed by social purposes.[4]

In practice, that meant that all allocation decisions were to be made by the government or its agencies. The importance of raising resources for development was, of course,

[4]NITI Aayog, *Approach to the Second Five Year Plan*, https://bit.ly/33Ydg2S, accessed on 24 January 2022.

considered important. However, the primary emphasis was to be on increasing the domestic savings rate by suppressing consumption and appropriating profits through ownership of commercial enterprises. Accelerated capital accumulation through these means was considered to be the key to development. In a celebrated observation which guided many a planner and policymaker in developing countries, Professor W. Arthur Lewis observed that:

> The central problem in the theory of economic development is to understand the process by which a community which was previously saving and investing 4 or 5 per cent of its national income or less, converts itself to an economy where voluntary saving is running at about 12 to 15 per cent of national income or more. This is the central problem because the central fact of economic development is rapid capital accumulation (including knowledge and skills with 'capital'.[5]

In the process of capital accumulation, the role of the financial system was essentially limited, as allocation decisions were to be made by the central planning authorities and not by the financial markets. To a large extent, the financial system also had a limited role in providing incentives for savings and capital accumulation as interest rates were controlled, and generally 'repressed', and household savings were pre-empted through high levels of statutory reserve and liquidity

---

[5]Lewis, W.A., *Economic Development with Unlimited Supplies of Labour*, Manchester School, Vol. 22, 1954, p. 10, https://bit.ly/3rK6Dtd, accessed on 24 January 2022.

ratio. New banks and financial institutions were set up, and old ones were taken over, in order to act primarily as deposit-taking agencies and providers of credit and finance for designated and centrally determined purposes.

The above development paradigm has, of course, shifted rather sharply in recent years. Almost all the developing countries are moving towards a more market-determined strategy of development. There are several factors that have contributed to this change in perception. The most important reason for questioning the earlier strategy was the simple fact that actual results in terms of growth of incomes or industrial development were well below expectations. Despite the substantial increase in the domestic savings rates in several countries, including India, the growth rate of incomes was relatively low. While saving rates were rising, so were capital–output ratios because of inefficiencies in the allocation and use of resources. The period of relatively low growth also coincided with a period of virtually persistent and recurring balance-of-payments crises. Thus, paradoxically, a strategy that was expected to reduce dependency on foreign aid and foreign trade actually resulted in greater dependence on aid and emergency assistance from abroad.

An equally important factor contributing to the change in perceptions was the astonishing success of Japan and the East Asian countries in accelerating their growth rates by relying on the market-oriented pattern of industrialization (with, of course, varying degrees of 'guidance' by the State). Japan's per capita growth rate of 8 per cent per annum during 1953–73 was unprecedented in the history of economic development. No economy had ever grown that fast before, and Japan emerged from the ruins of war to become the world's second-largest economy. Similar was the record of industrialization in East Asia, particularly in countries such as Hong Kong, Singapore, Taiwan and South Korea. In the 1950s, their per capita incomes or the degree of industrialization was no different from those of the rest of Asia. However, within a period of 30 years, they were able to catch up with the industrialized countries of the West. A final and decisive development leading to the demise of the old strategy was the collapse of the Soviet Union and the acceptance of market-led development strategies by all countries of Eastern Europe.

The change in the development paradigm also led to a change in the perception about the role of the financial system in development. It became clear that liberalization of product markets also requires a well-functioning financial system for mobilization and allocation of savings. Banks, capital markets and financial institutions were no longer seen as mere conduits for channelling savings in predetermined directions, but rather as important instruments for allocating savings among alternative investment choices according to their relative efficiency.

After the onset of the Asian crisis in mid-1997, there was a further change in the perception about the role of the financial system in development. Earlier, the real economy was supposed to lead and shape the financial system. In the late 1990s, proper development of the financial system was no longer regarded as an 'ancillary' or an adjunct to the development of the real sector, but as a necessary precondition for growth.

The above developments in the real world were supported by findings in the theoretical literature, which demonstrated the critical role of the financial system in the growth process. The financial liberalization literature developed in the 1970s and 1980s stressed the costs of 'financial repression', particularly interest rate and exchange rate controls which restricted growth of financial intermediation and the real rate of economic growth. These findings were buttressed by the emergence of endogenous growth literature, which emphasized the importance of the financial market as a source of innovation and productivity growth. It was demonstrated that an efficient and well-functioning financial system contributed to economic growth by raising the level of saving and investment as well as the productivity of capital.

The change in the perception about the role of the financial system in development during the 1990s was combined with a fair amount of debate on the nature and characteristics of financial markets as distinguished from products or factor markets. Were financial markets special? Did they require a different set of regulatory or supervisory regimes? What were the relative roles of international and domestic institutions and supervisory regimes in ensuring the viability and integrity of the financial system in a particular country in the context of globalization or 'globality', as some preferred to call it?

Currently, financial markets have indeed certain special

characteristics. The most important of these is the large volume of transactions and the speed with which financial resources can move from one market to another, and from one instrument to another. A related characteristic is a scope for instant connectivity between different markets and between different types of instruments. Financial transactions can be highly leveraged and the risk of failure can be transferred by actual decision makers to innocent bystanders.

Another interesting characteristic of these markets is the role of financial intermediaries. There are segments of financial markets, such as stock markets and bond markets, where savers themselves make the decision about when and where their money can be used. Markets are, however, also dominated by financial intermediaries (such as banks, provident funds, pension funds, mutual funds and so on), which take investment decisions as well as risks on behalf of their depositors. Yet another important characteristic of financial markets is the so-called 'negative' externalities associated with them. A failure in any one segment of these markets may affect all other segments of the market, including the non-financial markets.

Financial markets are also highly susceptible to 'self-fulfilling' prophecy or expectations. Sometimes, 'self-fulfilling' expectations can lead to panic as the behaviour of a limited group of operators gets generalized. Noted economist Jagdish N. Bhagwati has described the classic case of a self-fulfilling prophecy with reference to the behaviour of exchange rates dating back to the 1960s. He illustrates this particular feature of the foreign exchange market:

> Let the objective reality initially be that the dollar will not depreciate. But suppose that speculators expect the opposite, and move out of the dollar, depreciating it. If the reality were independent of the actions of the speculators, the dollar would go up again, and the market would have chastised and ruined the speculators. But it may well be that as the dollar falls initially with the speculation, wages and hence prices rise in sympathy. If so, the objective reality would itself have changed, legitimating the devaluation of the dollar in view of the speculation-induced rise of prices. Such self-justifying speculation shapes its own reality.[6]

In view of the externalities, volatility and certain other special characteristics, it is generally agreed that financial markets have to be closely monitored and supervised. It has also been the past experience that, in view of the growing integration of worldwide financial markets, failure and vulnerability in the domestic market in a particular country can have international implications. Similarly, problems in the external markets can create difficult problems for the functioning of the domestic markets, even if the country concerned was following prudent macroeconomic policies. This close relationship between the two markets—domestic

---

[6]Bhagwati, Jagdish N., *A Stream of Windows: Unsettling Reflections on Trade, Immigration, and Democracy*, The MIT Press, Cambridge, 1998, p. 453.

and external—raises the question of their appropriate duties and responsibilities, as well as those of domestic supervisory authorities and international financial institutions. Most of these issues have come to the fore in the context of the East Asian crisis and subsequent developments in certain other countries, such as Russia and Brazil.

Lessons from the Asian Crisis

Much has been said and written about the causes of the Asian crisis and its aftermath. The literature is voluminous, and as impressive as the earlier literature on the 'Asian miracle', and raises the obvious question of what developing countries must learn from their successes. This section highlights some aspects of the Asian crisis which have a bearing on the understanding of the relationship between finance and development, and the lessons that countries like India need to keep in view in order to avoid having to go through similar devastating experiences in the future.

An important point to remember in this context is that even relatively small mistakes in the conduct of macroeconomic or exchange rate policies can sometimes lead to big crises. The Asian experience is certainly mixed, and the magnitude of macroeconomic and other policy failures in different East Asian countries was not the same. However, in several of them, the degree of deviation from the best practices or prudent policies was relatively small. It may be that they persisted with the defence of the pegged exchange rates for a week or two longer than was desirable, or it may be that they did not take corrective monetary or fiscal action early enough. However, the devastation and the pain that their economies went through because of these policy mistakes were sizeable and unprecedented. This, incidentally, was also the experience of Mexico and Argentina in early 1995, when a major emerging crisis was brought under a semblance of control by a massive international rescue effort launched by the International Monetary Fund (IMF), the US and the World Bank. It is no coincidence that in all these cases—in East Asia as well as in Mexico and Argentina—the proximate cause was the relatively sudden reversal of capital flows on which these economies had become excessively dependent. It had taken a relatively long time to build a climate of confidence, and for capital inflows to rise gradually. However, it took no time for this confidence to be dissipated and for foreign capital to disappear. It is also interesting to note that the major reversal was not only on account of foreign lenders or investors but also on account of resident holders of domestic assets who rushed to encash or convert their holdings into foreign currency.

The point is simply that handling capital flows is not easy. While capital account liberalization and large capital movements have brought considerable growth benefits, they have also brought with them greater potential for volatility in asset prices and financial markets, including forex markets. This can cause unanticipated damage to the real economy during periods of uncertainty about the future economic or political outlook. As mentioned earlier, adverse expectations about a country's future during periods of uncertainty can often become 'self-fulfilling'. The fact that such volatility can be aggravated by a weak financial system, leading to severe developmental problems, has also to be borne in mind. The lesson from the Mexican or East Asian episodes is not an argument against capital flows or capital account convertibility. It is about careful and judicious handling of such flows and about the pace of movement towards capital account liberalization for residents. It is also about building domestic safety nets; for example, by keeping the level of liquid foreign exchange reserves high in relation to short-term external obligations.

It cannot be denied that, despite the earlier spectacular successes, the financial systems of East Asian countries were characterized by several weaknesses. Thus, banks were not subject to effective prudential regulation and supervision. Credit expansion in these countries was large and banks took untenable positions in real estate and other unproductive assets, and in the process building up large asset–liability and currency mismatches. Banks had also built up huge off-balance sheet liabilities, which moved on to the balance sheet once there was adversity. Cross-border interbank positions were also large. Non-banking financial companies contributed to the crisis as these were subject to little or no regulation.

Corporates were also highly leveraged. External debt was available at low interest rates and the fixed exchange rates in these countries offered them a false sense of complacency, encouraging them to hold large unhedged positions. External debt was high, short term, leveraged and concentrated in the private sector. Thus, on the whole, there was an inherent vulnerability in the financial sector, and once the expectation turned adverse, this vulnerability easily translated itself into a state of panic. Standards of accounting practices, financial reporting and disclosure norms were somewhat inadequate in these countries. There was a lack of transparency in the operations of market participants as well as the central banks in some cases.

Events in East Asia have certainly highlighted the two-way interaction between the financial sector and development and the need for an appropriate policy framework. Improving the efficiency of the financial sector through market-based reforms is an important concern of the new development paradigm. However, this has to be accompanied by policies, practices and a certain amount of restraints that strengthen the financial system towards stability so that growth becomes sustainable. At the same time, proper emphasis has to be placed on growth policies that do not give rise to problems that engender systemic instability in the financial sector (e.g. a large fiscal deficit).

A related issue is that of striking an appropriate balance between financial regulation and market freedom. While freedom is essential to foster efficiency, it also raises an equally important question of an appropriate regulatory framework given the wide divergence between private and social interests in ensuring the stability of the financial system. Hence, a proper system of regulation relating to prudent risk limits, short-term foreign borrowing and the degree of tolerable maturity mismatches in the banking system assumes critical importance for minimizing risks to the stability of the financial system.

The most important lesson emerging from the Asian crisis, in my view, is the need to be vigilant about domestic and international developments which may impinge on a country's financial relations with the rest of the world. The process of integration of worldwide financial markets has resulted in product innovation and greater efficiency, but it has also made developing countries subject to greater vulnerability and new risks. Strong fundamentals alone cannot provide full immunity from a crisis. There is a need to take early preventive action, build firewalls and keep some safety nets handy. It is also clear that when things are going well, the rest of the world shares the prosperity. However, when things go wrong, the price has to be paid primarily by the country concerned. It is, therefore, an important responsibility of the countries themselves to put in place an efficient, prudential and safe financial system that can aid and protect the development process at all times—good and bad.

The Indian Experience

This section deals with financial sector reforms in India from the perspective of past experience, the present stage of development and some issues for the future against the backdrop of the lessons from the Asian crisis.

The Past

As mentioned earlier in the book, for nearly 40 years after Independence, India's development strategy laid stress on state-guided development initiatives. The primary role was assigned to the state and its agencies for mobilization as well as allocation of savings. It was not until the Eighth Five-Year Plan (1992–97) that the role of the financial sector and financial markets was given explicit recognition in the development strategy. The emphasis on accelerating investment rate through state intervention in a number of key areas meant channelling credit to certain preferential sectors at subsidized interest rates, exercising public ownership control on banks and restricting their activities through policy prescriptions. Some of the typical features that got built into this system were the directed lending programme with high levels of cash reserve ratio and statutory liquidity ratio, ceiling on deposit and lending rate, lending to priority sectors, branch licencing, and detailed regulation of banks' loan and investment portfolios.

With regards to external finance, India relied essentially on bilateral and multilateral official development assistance and did not encourage private external capital inflows as a way to supplement domestic savings. The exchange rate was administered and there was extensive control over all the foreign exchange transactions, which were subject to approval on a case-by-case basis. Owing to the pervasive exchange controls, the Indian financial system remained largely insulated from international markets. This, however, did not prevent India from suffering regular balance-of-payments crises year after year and becoming increasingly dependent on aid flows or credits from the IMF.

As a consequence, the financial system faced little to no competition—either domestic or foreign—and costs and efficiency of transactions were not its main concerns. Productivity was generally poor and profitability low. The system was also subject to limited accountability. By the beginning of the 1990s, it became evident that the system could not be sustained without a thorough revamping of its operations.

The balance-of-payments crisis during 1990–91 provided the trigger point of reform in several sectors, including the financial sector. The reform initiatives in the financial sector started with the government appointing two committees: one on the balance of payments, under the chairmanship of Dr C. Rangarajan, which went into liberalization of policies in the external sector, and the second, on the financial systems, under the chairmanship of M. Narasimham, which deliberated on domestic financial sector reforms. The reform programme in the financial sector after 1992 largely followed the broad approach set out by these two committees, supplemented by the Narasimham Committee II, which was set up in 1998.

The Present

In so far as the 'arithmeticals' of reform in the financial sector—to use a phrase used by the Narasimham Committee—is concerned, significant progress was made in the 1990s. There was a steady decline in the level of resource pre-emption from the banking system. Both cash reserve ratio and statutory liquidity ratio were reduced from their high levels of 15 per cent and 38.5 per cent, respectively, in 1991–92 to 9 per cent and 25 per cent, respectively, in 1999. Interest rates in various segments of financial markets were deregulated in a phased manner. This had preceded the abolition of control on capital issues and the freeing of interest rates on private bonds and debentures. While the government borrowing rates were market-determined, there was a gradual phasing out of interest rate subsidies on bank loans. Wide-ranging reforms were initiated to develop and deepen the government securities market, money market, capital market and foreign exchange market. The Bank Rate was reactivated, regular short-term Repos at a pre-announced rate were being conducted and a system of prime lending rate was introduced to provide direction to the movement of interest rates in the credit market.

In the sphere of external financial policy, while the exchange rate has been market-determined, over the years, there was a progressive liberalization of foreign direct and portfolio investment and approval procedures were considerably simplified. As a result, there have been minimum restrictions on the inflow of capital into the economy, or its repatriation and servicing. There has also been a significant liberalization of policy regarding industry's access to foreign equity and borrowing through long-term debt instruments. The banking sector has been given a greater degree of freedom with regard to raising funds abroad and managing their external liability, subject to prudential guidelines. The end result of all these and other reforms has been the growing integration among various segments of financial markets, closer convergence of the Indian financial system with practices prevailing in international financial markets, and greater opportunity for investors to access both domestic and international markets. At the same time, care has been taken to avoid excessive short-term external liability and asset–liability mismatches.

Competitive condition in the banking industry has been facilitated by relaxing entry and exit norms and permitting public-sector banks to raise additional capital from the market (up to a certain level). While public-sector banks continue to be predominant, the changing competitive environment in the banking sector has made a significant difference to banking practices and disclosure requirements.

Prudential regulation and supervision have formed a critical component of the financial sector reform programme. India has adopted international prudential norms and practices with regard to capital adequacy, income recognition, provisioning requirement and supervision. These norms have been progressively tightened over the years, particularly against the backdrop of the Asian crisis. The required capital adequacy ratio has been increased to 9 per cent, from 8 per cent, in the banking sector. The mark-to-market practice for valuation of government securities has been gradually enhanced from 30 per cent in 1992–93 to 75 per cent by 1999–2000. A further refinement, in line with international best practices, in the valuation and classification of investments by banks is also under consideration. As a further prudential measure against credit and market risks, risk weights have been made applicable to government and other securities to take account of price variations.

An attempt has also been made to avoid the problems arising from connected lending. There have been regulations that limit the exposure of individual banks and non-banking finance companies to any particular borrower or groups of borrowers. There are restrictions on banking system's exposure to equity and lending against equity as collateral, and its exposure to real estate is very limited. Prudent limits have been placed on the financial system and the corporate sector as far as external borrowing is concerned.

In the area of supervision, a full-fledged institutional mechanism has been developed keeping in view the needs of a strong and stable financial system. The system of off-site surveillance has been combined with periodical on-site supervision for monitoring the risk profile of banks and their compliance with prudential guidelines. The Basel Core Principles for Effective Banking Supervision is substantially being adhered to. The RBI's regulatory and supervisory responsibility has also been widened to include financial institutions and non-banking financial companies.

As a result of these and other measures, some progress in the performance of the Indian banking system is noticeable in 1990. The trend in erosion of profit and capital base has been reversed. The net profits of the public-sector banks, as a percentage of their total assets, averaged 0.4 per cent during 1994–95 to 1998–99, against the loss of about 1 per cent in 1992–93 and 1993–94. The gross non-performing assets of public-sector banks (without allowing for provisions) as per cent of total assets had declined from about 12 per cent in 1992–93 to about 7 per cent in 1998–99. As of March 1999, all public-sector banks except one had achieved capital adequacy ratios exceeding the prescribed norm of 8 per cent. The improved performance has enabled most of the banks to meet their capital requirement from internal resources and the market without dependence on budgetary support.

The consolidation of the financial system in the 1990s has led to increased resilience of the Indian economy to external crisis. This has been evident from the muted impact of the Asian crisis on the Indian financial markets. Since then, there has been a constant effort to enhance the regulatory and supervisory standards in conformity with international standards.

To sum up, it is clear that, thanks to the guidance provided by committees headed by Dr Rangarajan and Shri Narasimham, there has been a significant progress in broadening and strengthening of India's financial system. The task is, however, far from complete. Some of the areas, which require priority consideration in the future, are discussed below.

The Future

The agenda for the future is long. Fortunately, there has been a widespread interest and debate among experts and market participants on various aspects of financial reform which has enabled India to chart out a path which is best suited to enhance growth with financial stability. In this section, a few areas which deserve priority in the near future are highlighted.

First and foremost, it is necessary to continue with the process of strengthening prudential, provisioning and capitalization norms and bring them in line with best international standards. It is equally important to continue with efforts to introduce maximum transparency, disclosure and accountability so that investors and counterparties to financial transactions can take their decisions based on full information and their own assessment of market and other risks. Tighter and tougher prudential standards will no doubt cause some pain and impose greater responsibility on banks and other financial institutions. However, as mentioned earlier, given the new international focus and externalities and linkages involved, the regulation of the financial sector is no longer a matter of choice or a matter of domestic concern alone. Over a period of time, it is likely that the willingness of the rest of the world to do financial business—either by way of trade credit, direct investments or other types of investments and loans—will depend on their confidence in financial practices. India must remain ahead of the curve in its prudential management.

The level of non-performing assets (NPAs) of the banking system in India has shown some improvement in recent years, but it is still too high. Part of the problem in resolving this issue is the carry-over of old NPAs in certain declining sectors of industry. The Narasimham Committee and the Verma Committee Report on Weak Public Sector Banks have looked into the problems of weak banks and have made certain recommendations which are under consideration of the government and the RBI. These are also being widely debated, so that an acceptable long-term solution can be evolved. Leaving aside the problem of weak banks, in profitable banks too, the NPA levels are still high. A vigorous effort needs to be made by these banks to strengthen their internal control and risk management systems, and to set up early warning signals for timely detection and corrective action. The resolution of the NPA problem also requires greater accountability on the part of corporates, greater disclosures in the case of defaults and an efficient credit information system.

The problem of NPAs is also tied up with the issue of legal reform. This is an area which requires urgent consideration as the existing system, involving substantial delays in arriving at a legal solution of disputes, is simply not tenable. It is hoped that some of the initiatives taken by the government, such as establishing more Debt Recovery Tribunals and setting up of Settlement Advisory Committees in banks, would help. However, there is an urgent need to institute a proper legal framework to ensure expeditious recovery of debt and give adequate legal powers to banks to effect property transfers.

In order to allow for growth in their assets in line with real growth in the economy, banks and financial institutions would need to increase their capitalization quite substantially in the next few years. In the 1990s, the minimum shareholding by the RBI in the State Bank of India (SBI), prescribed by legislation, was set at 55 per cent. The minimum percentage of shareholding by the government in public-sector banks is 51 per cent. So far, a number of strong banks have been able to access capital markets to meet their capitalization requirements in line with prudential guidelines. Some of these banks, including the SBI, now have limited scope to raise further capital from the market within the prescribed floor of the RBI and government shareholdings. If the risk-weighted assets of these banks grow in line with the growth in the economy in the next five years, additional capital requirements of these banks may exceed ₹10,000 crore. As against this requirement, the headroom available for these banks to raise capital from the market is less than ₹1,000 crore. After allowing for additional infusion of reserve capital through internal generation and access to subordinated debt, the gap between their additional capital requirement and the leeway available to raise capital from the market will still remain quite sizeable.

In this situation, an issue that needs to be debated and resolved is whether this gap should be filled by contribution from the RBI (in the case of SBI) and the government (in the case of other public-sector banks) or whether legislative ceiling for capital subscribed by the public should be raised. The provision of additional capital by the RBI is tantamount to additional monetization, and its monetary impact is equivalent to that of printing additional currency. Contribution to banks' capital by the government has a similar effect as it will add to the government's deficit, which is already high. The government, in any case, would need to provide additional capital to weak banks, which are not in a position to raise capital on their own. Does it make economic or fiscal sense to add to this burden further? On balance, there seems to be a strong case for raising the legislative ceiling for market participation in equity capital of public-sector banks.

At the same time, it has to be recognized that, in view of the need to give adequate attention to agricultural credit and rural banking and also to maintain public confidence in the safety of banks, the public-sector character of these banks need not be given up. Keeping these considerations in view, i.e. those of allowing greater access to markets while at the same time maintaining the public-sector character of banks presently owned by the government or the RBI, it may be necessary to prescribe a maximum (at a suitably low level) for shareholding by any single individual or a corporate in public-sector banks. The government may also retain the pre-emptive right to appoint, if it wishes, the chief executive and the majority of the board members in public-sector banks.

Over the years, progressive liberalization of financial markets and institutional reforms have led to growing interlinkages among various segments of financial markets. The emergence of different types of financial intermediaries, in addition to banks and financial institutions, is healthy and desirable. In the event of unanticipated problems, a diversified structure contributes to greater stability of the financial system. In India, while there has been progress in developing various segments of the markets, including money and debt markets, the depth of these markets remains low and the volumes as well as the number of participants are not very large. An important priority for the future is to develop the depth and breadth of these markets and to allow multiplicity of intermediation possibilities with different risks and leverage profiles. The RBI will continue to work with financial experts and market participants to develop an appropriate procedural and policy framework to move in this direction.

India also has to devise measures to make the interest rate structure more flexible in order to take account of changes in economic cycles and the inflation outlook. At present, for reasons which were highlighted in the Mid-term Review of Monetary and Credit Policy in October 1999, there are several constraints which limit the flexibility of interest rates in the banking sector as well as the rest of the financial sector. Given the fact that some of these constraints are deeply embedded in historical practices, consumer preference and public-sector requirements, it may take some time to fully meet this objective. However, the process should begin now.

Conclusion

The change in the development paradigm from a largely state-directed strategy to a market-oriented one, and the unsatisfactory results of the earlier strategy, have highlighted the role of the financial system in efficient mobilization and allocation of a society's savings. All over the developing world, in the 1990s, there was intense activity in reviewing the structure of the financial markets and taking measures to liberalize and broaden them.

Against this background, and that of past dissatisfactions with the old strategy, it is interesting to note that the record of development in the 1990s has been a highly disappointing one for the developing world as a whole, with two important exceptions—India and China. The 1990s—the period of the triumph of capitalism and financial liberalization—had a growth rate of only 3.2 per cent in world output which was lower than the average of 3.9 per cent in the 1970s and not much different from the growth rate of 3.4 per cent in the 1980s. This period also had a large number of currency crises (from the Exchange Rate Mechanism [ERM] crisis in Europe in the early part of the decade to the Mexican, Russian, Asian and the Brazilian crises later). This period also saw substantial swings in exchange rates (including the exchange rate of two leading currencies: the dollar and the yen); run-ups in asset prices followed by sharp collapse (for example, in Japan, Nordic countries and Asia) and banking crises in almost all the regions of the world.

The purpose of drawing attention to this rather disheartening record is not that India should return to the old, failed strategy. Nor is it to suggest that financial liberalization or development of the financial markets is unnecessary. The old strategy collapsed under the weight of its own excesses and contradictions. Similarly, there is no doubt that financial reform and liberalization of markets are necessary, essential and desirable to derive the maximum advantage from the momentous changes that are taking place in technology, international movement of capital and comparative advantage of nations. The purpose of highlighting some of the problems that have emerged in the world economy in the 1990s is to underscore simply one point: that no developing country should confuse 'means' with 'ends'. Financial reforms and liberalization of markets are the means to an end, and not ends in themselves. The final objective of a successful development strategy remains what it has always been—a sustained and rising income for all the people, and removal of poverty, deprivation and illiteracy within a reasonable period of time.

While India must remain steadfast in the pursuit of financial sector reforms, the success of this process should not be viewed from the angle of how much freedom it allows to the market players. The real test is how much benefit all this brings in terms of development, including greater employment opportunities and poverty alleviation for those who do not participate in the markets. It will also be wrong to view financial reforms as an antithesis of the government's role in development or the role of public policy in widening social choices and opportunities. In developing countries, with massive illiteracy and underdevelopment of infrastructure, the government should continue to have an important and crucial role in creating the necessary conditions for growth through investments in areas such as education, healthcare, water supply, irrigation and infrastructure. These and similar tasks cannot be fully taken over by the market. Successful financial reforms must result in strengthening the ability of governments to do what they need to do by helping to generate higher growth, higher revenues and higher productivity. In developed countries, the so-called 'potential output' of the economy, whatever its estimated level, can be left to be realized by changing the parameters of financial and monetary policy. In developing countries, the main challenge is to raise the level of potential output by removing the constraints of infrastructure and low human resource development.

Which Way Now?

The financial system functions on trust and it is incumbent on the RBI and other financial regulators to ensure that the system works smoothly. A lack of trust in the system can adversely affect financial intermediation, impeding the flow of savings to the productive sectors of the economy. To minimize financial stability risks, the government and the banking regulator would have to work at multiple levels. For one, it is important to see to it that financial institutions adhere to the best governance standards. To ensure this, the regulator itself will have to build adequate institutional capacity. It is possible that there will be some rogue elements who would want to game the system, but the regulator should be in a position to control them in time.

Clearly, the RBI needs to improve its audit processes for both banks and non-banking financial companies. Failure on this count can put the entire financial system at risk.

Alongside financial reform and development of markets, it is essential that the country's attention must also turn to fiscal empowerment of the state and improvement in public administration. More than 74 years after Independence, India's public offices, including public-sector institutions, are still deficient in respect of delivery of services or in the efficient discharge of essential functions. A thorough review of the institutional framework, rules, regulations and accountability of the administrative organs of the state is now essential. The focus has to be on what they do for the people, and not on what they do for themselves. If our public institutions, including those in the field of education and healthcare, are unable to overcome their inertia, alternative modalities have to be found by the government for delivering these and other services.

Many of the functions of the state are now left undone or inefficiently done because of financial stringency at the Centre as well as in the states. The dependence on borrowings to finance even essential expenditure has been increasing year after year, leading to a vulnerable and unsustainable fiscal situation. Without adequate finance, the state cannot fulfill its developmental role or remove the constraints to the country's potential output. Pioneering work has been done by several research institutions, as well as by the central and several state governments, to identify measures that need to be taken to reinvigorate the fiscal system.

With a revitalized fiscal situation and further progress in establishing a forward-looking, strong and stable financial system in India, we can truly hope for a century of development, high growth and poverty alleviation.

Section 3

POLITICS

8

THE POLITICS OF POWER

There have been some recent developments in the institutional framework, which have considerably reduced the effectiveness of India's democratic system in serving the people. Democracy, like any other form of government, confers enormous powers on those who are elected or appointed to offices of the State. The great advantage of a democratic form of government, as compared with more authoritarian regimes, is the accountability of elected representatives to the people, particularly at the time of periodic elections. Unfortunately, in India, while elections are free and fair, they have not been able to get men of power to live 'for' the public rather than 'off' the public. This was not always the case, and even today, there are several honourable exceptions among politicians who have given up their successful professional careers to serve the people. However, as a rule, there is a common and widely shared perception that politics is now a profession of choice for those who enjoy the benefits of power and the various immunities that it confers.

All parties, old and new, nominate some persons with a history of criminal offences or other legal violations to contest elections. The governments in all states (with perhaps a couple of exceptions) have cabinets that include a fair number of such persons in charge of sensitive ministries. In recent years, this has been the case at the Centre too. A common defence of this practice is that persons with criminal records have been elected 'by the people'. Therefore, in a government 'of the people', they cannot be denied their just rewards. Interestingly and quite ironically, this argument does not apply to any other public servant or to members of any other profession. The special position accorded to criminals in political life has resulted in an interesting consequence: an increase in the 'demand' for entry into politics by those whose cases are pending in judicial courts at different levels.

The organizational structure of political power is 'pyramidal' in shape, as mentioned earlier. It is wide at the base or the grassroots, where the number of persons elected to political offices such as gram panchayats is large in number and entry is relatively free. However, the number of such offices shrinks drastically at the district, state or Union levels. The size of the electorate increases exponentially as one moves higher up the ladder, while the number of political constituencies and offices become fewer. The higher the level of an office, the pyramidal structure of political power increases the mismatch between supply and demand for that office and increases its scarcity value.

This phenomenon partly explains why at higher political levels, entry into politics has become more restrictive. Access to politics at the higher levels (with some honourable exceptions) is now available only to persons with sufficient 'clout', in terms of family connections, money, ethnic and caste loyalty and/or coercive power. Competitive politics has also made electoral politics expensive, which has further reduced its accessibility to the average person who lacks adequate means, power and command over a community's resources.

Another consequence of the high value attached to scarce political power is the emergence of leaders who enjoy a certain amount of 'monopoly' in the use of power. This explains the virtual disappearance of inner-party democracy from the Indian political scene. Most parties, again with a few exceptions, have leaders who alone (or with the help of some trusted aides) decide who will fight elections, who will join the cabinet, and who will get nominated to various political and government offices. In case there is a threat to the power of a leader from another aspiring member of the same party, that member is likely to be expelled or declared persona non grata. Alternatively, if that aspiring member has adequate political strength and following, the original party is likely to be split. Parties may also be split from time to time for other reasons, such as joining a coalition in power or accepting the inducements offered by an aspirant with money or clout. As a result, the number of parties vigorously contesting elections shows an increase over time, with most parties winning only a few seats.

As one moves up the political pyramid, the 'scope' of power available to leaders also increases, further enhancing the scarcity value of power and demand for such offices at higher levels. At the village level, the principal responsibilities entrusted to political representatives are relatively few. These include identification of beneficiaries under poverty alleviation and employment-generation schemes, among others. However, they have very little budgetary or financial powers to raise resources, and the bulk of fiscal resources for poverty-alleviation programmes are allocated by the central and state governments. Village-level panchayats also generally have no role in the delivery of education and healthcare services to residents. The operation of primary or secondary schools and public health centres continues to remain under the control of state government officials and their political masters.

The scope of powers available to political leaders increases enormously at the state and central levels. At the state level, in addition to a 100-plus centrally sponsored poverty alleviation and other schemes, there are a large number of infrastructure projects under management or construction. Another important source of financial power is the state co-operative and primary co-operative societies, which are fully or largely under the control of political representatives. In addition, there are numerous public-sector commercial or service organizations which have been set up by the state governments and are directly under the control of political leaders in administrative ministries. State governments also have practically unlimited powers to establish new agencies and public-sector organizations, with separate budgets and separate management structures.

At the Centre, of course, the entire governance machinery of the country is under the control and direction of political leaders. Thus, the predominant proportion of fiscal powers (including exclusive jurisdiction over custom tariffs and corporate taxation), the large public-sector undertakings in important sectors of the economy (such as banks, insurance, petroleum, food procurement and food distribution) and control over the allocation of national resources (including investment in crucial sectors, such as power, roads, aviation and ports) are under their control and direction. All matters relating to defence and external affairs, including defence procurement, are the exclusive preserve of the central government.

A development that has considerably increased the power of party leaders at the Centre, at the cost of state legislatures, is the amendment in the eligibility criteria of candidates for election to the Rajya Sabha (the so-called 'Council of States' at the Centre). Earlier, only people resident in a state were eligible for election by that state's legislature to the Rajya Sabha. These elections were through a secret ballot, so that legislators could exercise their franchise freely. Recently, the residence criterion as well as the provision of secret voting have been withdrawn through legislative amendments to the applicable rules. The central party leaders are empowered to nominate any person of their choice from anywhere in the country to represent a state in the Rajya Sabha. As the voting by legislators is open and subject to a whip, the legislators have practically no choice in choosing their representatives. In principle, the membership of the Rajya Sabha is now open to any person without any knowledge of the problems pertaining to or having any connection with the state that they are expected to represent in the Council of States. As the field is wide open and the number of seats is limited, after these amendments, the scarcity value of Rajya Sabha seats has also increased substantially.

It is well known that politicians, as representatives of the people, enjoy a great deal of power in all spheres of public life. This, after all, is the essence of democracy. The government is expected to work in the interest of the people, and it is their representatives who have to ensure that happens. Unfortunately, this proposition, which is entirely valid in theory, has become highly vitiated in practice, particularly in democracies where governments enjoy substantial power over the allocation of resources in the economy, including the savings of ordinary people and investments by the public and private sectors. This is true of India too, despite the economic reforms of the 1990s. For example, individual ministers in different ministries are fully empowered to change tax concessions or tax rates (with the pro forma approval of Parliament and the cabinet), or to change educational or urban development policy (with or without the cabinet's approval).

The vast scope of political power, its rising scarcity value and its pyramidal organization structure highlight the need for political reforms in the future without compromising on socio-economic priorities. The enormous discretionary powers available to politicians at different levels of society has had several unintended consequences, including diversion of fiscal resources for the benefit of the better-off sections of society at the expense of the poor, uneconomic selection of projects, increase in bureaucratic complexity and criminalization of politics. These adverse economic, developmental and social effects of enormous political power, in an environment of fiscal stringency, judicial delays and administrative apathy, are not widely appreciated. Some of these adverse effects are discussed below.

In a large country like ours, the situation varies a great deal from one state to another. Even within the same state, there are significant variations in the effective implementation of programmes and in the exercise of political power in the allocation of resources. Some states, under enlightened leadership, do quite well from time to time, while others may remain mired in sloppy leadership and widespread diversionary practices. Similarly, as mentioned, not all politicians are alike in their orientation. Several of them work selflessly to maximize the public good even under the most adverse circumstances.

Centralization of Political Power

Generally, 'political favouritism' is regarded as a legitimate exercise of power in furthering the interests of a particular group of constituents. With changes in coalitions and governments every few years, there is a mutuality of interest among political leaders in nurturing their constituencies, however antagonistic their political positions may be in public.

In India, one of the most remarkable political developments in the area of democratic decentralization was the passage of the 73rd Amendment to the Indian constitution in 1993. As is well known, this amendment created a new tier of local government which, by 2003, led to the constitution of as many as 2,35,000 new village-governing institutions, i.e. gram panchayats, staffed by over 2 million elected representatives. The gram panchayats function under an elected leader, the 'pradhan', who has the main executive responsibility of identifying beneficiaries. The pradhan of a gram panchayat is accountable to the gram sabha, a body in which all villagers are entitled to participate. This again is perhaps one of the most impressive experiments in the field of direct democracy anywhere in the world.

With higher levels of literacy and education in a village comes greater accountability of the pradhan to his/her constituents. Even then, some additional safeguards may be introduced by legislation to prevent the misuse of office and corruption among pradhans. Among such safeguards are the obligation to convene meetings of gram sabhas at least once every month, public disclosure of all decisions made by pradhans and strict enforcement of the Right to Information (RTI) Act.

Public Dissaving

It is well know that after India gained Independence, it adopted a highly controlled and centrally directed strategy of development. While the reasons for adopting a state-dominated development strategy are understandable given the background of colonial rule, by the mid-1950s, it had also become clear that the results of this strategy in generating self-reliant high growth were far below expectations. Looking back, it is hard to believe that for as long as four decades after 1950, India's growth rate averaged less than 4 per cent per annum and that per capita income growth was less than 2 per cent per annum. This was during a period when the developing world, including Sub-Saharan Africa and other least developed countries, showed a growth rate of 5.2 per cent per annum.

However, the most striking failure was not in terms of growth or even in terms of the precarious balance-of-payments situation. The most conspicuous development for which there is no alibi, and for which the responsibility lies squarely and indisputably with the deterioration in India's administrative system, is the erosion in public savings and the inability of the public sector to generate resources for investment or for the provision of public services.

It will be recalled that an important assumption in the choice of post-Independence development strategy was the generation of public savings, which could be used for higher and higher levels of investment. However, this did not happen, and the public sector, instead of being a generator of savings for the community's good, became a consumer of the community's savings. This reversal of roles had become evident by the early 1970s, and the process reached its culmination by the early 1980s. Since then, the government has begun to borrow not only to meet its own revenue expenditure but also to finance public-sector deficits and investments. The public sector, which had a commanding presence in almost all industrial sectors of the economy, particularly heavy industry, gradually became a net drain on society as a whole.

Against this background, an issue that deserves consideration is the reason for the political acceptance of dissaving at the expense of the larger public interest. The answer is not far to seek. Control over the public sector and the expansion of government expenditure, at the cost of people's savings, is a source of considerable political power. All government expenditure, however costly to society as a whole, benefits some individuals or sections of the people who are the beneficiaries of such expenditure. Since political leaders have the power to decide where to spend and which special groups to accord benefit, a higher level of government expenditure is always preferable to a cut in expenditure.

Another major source of power is the control over public-sector enterprises, which provide considerable employment opportunities. They are typically overstaffed and pay higher than market wages, particularly at clerical levels with strong unions. Public enterprises are also dominant in a number of important sectors of the economy, including the financial sector, which has a large number of public-sector banks and insurance companies with branches across

India. The top management and the boards of directors are appointed by administrative ministries with the approval of the appointments committee of the cabinet. There are selection boards for recommending names for consideration by the government for appointment as chairpersons, executive directors and board members. However, the final decision rests with the minister concerned and the Cabinet Committee.

There is nothing wrong with the above-mentioned procedure for selection and appointment, as it seeks to combine seniority and professional competence with political acceptance in the choice of personnel at top levels of management. However, in recent years, there has been a subtle change in the weights attached to the selection criteria. As appointments are subject to the discretion of the minister concerned, with little or no previous administrative experience in the ministry allotted to him/her, eligible contenders for the top offices (who also have short tenures before retirement) are more inclined to use political contacts to influence appointments in their favour. Control over public enterprises, particularly in the financial sector and in regions dominated by a few large manufacturing units, has become an important source of political power for leaders of parties represented in the government. There is a built-in incentive for setting up new public-sector units or branches since their location and the selection of staff at these locations are also subject to political discretion.

An advantage of control over public-sector enterprises is free publicity for ministers and other political dignitaries.

Newspapers in different languages are full of advertisements about inaugurations, milestones and conferences organized by public-sector units. There are hoardings on streets, at frequent intervals, to mark any event in which leaders are participating (including personal visits to states where their parties are in power). There are bridges and arches with paintings of leaders expressing their gratitude of the public for launching all kinds of new projects and programmes. All expenses for such personal publicity are generally paid for by public-sector enterprises, and occasionally by administrative ministries.

The issue here is not the public sector versus the private sector, or the ideological predilections in favour of a market-dominated strategy vis-à-vis state-dominated development strategy. Nor is it the case that all public enterprises perform inefficiently or that they do not contribute towards achieving the country's socio-economic goals. The point is simply that the exercise of political discretion in the functioning of public enterprises diminishes their potential contribution to the economy. There is no reasonable economic or ideological case for granting discretionary powers to political leaders in respect of appointments, management of commercial enterprises and allocation of resources. The socio-economic objectives can be more than adequately met by laying down appropriate policy guidelines, granting sufficient autonomy and entrusting the responsibility for high-level appointments, through transparent procedures, to official selection bodies.

Excessive Centralization

Owing to the pyramidal structure of political power, the end result is the over-centralization of administration rather than its decentralization. Many of the new ministries now have overlapping functions with existing ministries. In addition, there are ministries, offices and commissions with omnibus functions covering the entire government machinery, such as finance, planning, personnel and so on. This administrative structure at the Centre is replicated in the states. As most subjects are in the 'concurrent' list and/or involve the transfer of grants and loans from the Centre (e.g. power, irrigation and rural development), multiple ministries and agencies at the Centre and states are involved in all administrative decision-making and the implementation of programmes.

At the bottom of the pyramid are the administrative agencies at the district, town and village levels. Any work or programme at the level of the village or town is supposed to involve an elected body or a political representative in the decision-making process. Thus, as early as 1994 (after the 73rd Amendment to the Constitution), all concerned states had passed their own acts for implementing the decision to set up Panchayati Raj Institutions (PRIs) with financial and administrative powers. However, so far, states have not transferred most of the subjects or functions specified in the constitutional amendment to PRIs. In order to exercise direct authority in areas reserved for panchayats, different ministries of state governments have also been inclined to create parallel structures at the local and district levels by forming committees under their control.

In conclusion, it may be mentioned that there are some persons of exceptional talent and integrity in India's politics, who serve the country selflessly to promote the welfare of the public in general. There are also cases where political leaders have willingly renounced political power rather than seek it. It is also true that most other democracies, including those in Europe and the US, exhibit similar characteristics of power play as India. However, what is different here is the extent of economic power and domination over commercial activity by the government—directly or indirectly. It is this immense commercial power in the hands of political leaders which makes India different from other mature democracies. While democracy is its own reward and is precious to all citizens, there are costs attached to the unbridled exercise of power at the political level.

9

POLITICAL OPPORTUNISM

'Political opportunism' is a euphemism commonly used in the literature of behavioural economics to describe the bias among elected representatives at different levels to divest resources under a government programme to their own villages, constituencies or states. Generally, such 'political opportunism' is also regarded as a legitimate exercise of power in the interest of a particular group of constituencies. It is quite common for the leaders of different parties, when in power, to ensure that disproportionate benefits under various government programmes flow to their respective constituencies. A strong vested interest also develops among residents to re-elect their leaders. Leaders of state parties have the same preferences and derive the same benefits in terms of periodic re-elections. Interestingly, there is a tacit understanding among leaders of different political parties whether they are in power or in the Opposition, that their constituencies and interests would receive preferential treatment in the allocation of governmental resources.

On the face of it, most of this sounds reasonable and acceptable, but the cost of such preferential treatment for society as a whole can be substantial in view of the paucity of resources available under a particular programme. Thus, a particular constituency or area may get many more benefits irrespective of the number of impoverished among its residents or the average level of income. Therefore, it is common experience that the number of beneficiaries, say, under an employment-generation or poverty-alleviation programme, is disproportionately high in the constituency or state of a leader or minister leading the programme. A neighbouring state or district may be entitled to the same benefits, but is unlikely to get these even if it is poorer and more deficient with respect to the availability of public services. Another consequence is that political opportunism results in a substantial diversion of resources to those who are otherwise ineligible.

As was discussed earlier, the creation of the Constitution (73rd Amendment) Act, 1992 led to a new tier of local government which, in turn, led to the establishment of nearly 2,50,000 new village-governing institutions, i.e. gram panchayats, staffed by more than 2 million elected representatives. This is probably the largest number of persons elected to serve as people's representatives in any democracy in the world. Furthermore, as a remarkable experiment in affirmative action, the 73rd Amendment mandated that almost half of the elected positions be reserved for traditionally disadvantaged population groups (lower-caste groups and women). Although these village panchayats enjoy very limited financial powers, they have an overwhelming responsibility for beneficiary selection for government welfare programmes.

While political opportunism is also increasing at the level of the gram panchayat, the extent is much less than it is at the state level. Part of the reason for this is the visibility of the pradhan, and his/her direct accountability to the gram sabha. Also, the higher the level of literacy and education in a village, the greater is the accountability of the pradhan to his/her constituents.

As such, an appropriate measure for improving the performance of anti-poverty and employment-generation programmes should be to devolve the entire budgetary allocation to the gram panchayats without any direct involvement of state or central government agencies. So far, however, the Constitution (73rd Amendment) Act, 1992 has only led to the creation of another tier in the distribution of resources at the local level. State government agencies and central ministries remain just as involved in managing the programmes as they were before the establishment of gram panchayats. Indeed, there are separate 'panchayati raj' ministries in each of the states as well as at the Centre, and political leaders at these levels and their officers continue to have substantial supervisory and allocative powers over the gram panchayats.

Fiscal Disempowerment

In India, the people's representatives either in the state legislatures or in Parliament have practically no effective role in matters of taxation or allocation of expenditure under the government schemes. There is certainly a pro forma role in the sense that the budgets of governments have to be formally approved by the legislature. However, in practice, all the relevant decisions are made exclusively by a few top leaders in the government, and approved by the legislature as desired by the executive. The budget estimates, the revised estimates, the final accounts, the performance budgets, the outcome budgets and the reports of the Comptroller and Auditor General of India are regularly presented or tabled in Parliament. Sometimes, they are discussed. However, so far, there is no evidence that any person, agency or ministry has been held accountable for any deviation in budgetary receipts or expenditure or for any malpractices or failure to achieve the promised outcomes or targets.

Over time, while the number of programmes of all kinds has increased phenomenally, fiscal resources to finance such programmes have become more stringent at the Centre as well as in practically all the states. Another common feature of budgets at various levels (including districts and gram panchayats) is that most of the budget allocation under different heads is spent on the salaries of government officials responsible for the execution, supervision and monitoring of the various programmes. Capital expenditure for the improvement of infrastructure and/or revenue expenditure for providing monetary benefits or services to the people seldom exceeds 10 per cent of the budget allocations (except in a few programmes, which also suffer from substantial diversion of resources to unintended beneficiaries). In some states, the interest paid on accumulated state debt is almost as much as the total revenue collected by the state, leaving very little for expenditure on any development programme.

Political leaders and ministers have virtually unlimited powers to announce new schemes and programmes or replace and redesignate old programmes, but they have no fiscal room available to implement these programmes because of the vast amounts squandered on existing poorly planned programmes. Interestingly, fiscal disempowerment has led to increasing bureaucratic complexity and higher salary expenditure as procedures and checks to minimize budgetary outgoes on legitimate programme expenditure have multiplied. This is true in all spheres of government activity—from educational institutions at the highest levels to primary schools, from nationally reputed research hospitals to basic healthcare centres in villages, from transmission of power in metropolitan cities to non-electrified areas and so on.

The indifference of some state governments in implementing welfare, employment or other anti-poverty programmes after announcing them further accentuates the non-availability of adequate benefits to the poor. While ongoing projects remain unimplemented, part of the budgetary transfers remain unspent pending the inauguration of new schemes, appointment of new staff, payment of salaries, etc. This state of affairs, without accountability, is a direct consequence of the enormous budgetary powers enjoyed by political leaders in office. Ironically, these budgetary powers are conferred on them by most democratic constitutions on the ground that 'there should be no taxation without representation' and the belief that political leaders are the ones who alone are accountable to the people in deciding how budgetary resources should be spent. This noble principle is now honoured only in its breach.

Excessive Centralization

The pyramidal structure of political power has resulted in the over-centralization of administration. This has led to a substantial increase in the number of agencies—both horizontally and vertically—in the decision-making process. This has led to administrative delays and lack of accountability for non-performance. No ministry wants to give up its power. At the same time, new ministries have to be created in order to accommodate aspirants from the majority party or from some other parties that are part of ruling-party coalitions. Many of the new ministries have functions that overlap with those of the existing ministries.

The complexity of governance structure and the exercise of political and bureaucratic control at multiple levels of the administrative machinery is vividly illustrated in the Mahatma Gandhi National Rural Employment Guarantee Act (MGNREGA) that was adopted in 2005. While the objective of the Act is laudable, the bureaucratic structure for implementation of the programme is huge and unwieldy, involving several authorities at various levels of the political pyramid. Thus, in addition to several ministries of the central government and their counterparts in each state, the Act envisages as many as 10 or more agencies and committees at the Centre, state, district, block and village levels for implementation, monitoring, evaluation, coordination, grievance redressal and disbursement of funds.

The reluctance to devolve political power and the desire to create more new agencies is combined with two other features of an overburdened administrative structure. First, virtually all legislation proposed by the government at the Centre or in the states assigns residual and 'rule-making' powers to the concerned ministries. Such powers confer practically unlimited authority to frame new rules, amend old rules and create public-sector agencies under the Act. To acquire more power, in cases of doubt, the ministry can always propose adoption of a new Bill in place of an existing Act.

Second, the higher the position of a person in the political hierarchy, the greater is the level of ostentatious display of power and authority. Thus, political leaders surround themselves with security personnel, preferably armed with visible weapons, and travel in a convoy of cars. Such ostentation can, of course, be dismissed as frivolous. Unfortunately, however, it has an unintended effect on the politics of power. The loss of power, after elections or cabinet reshuffles, can lead to an acute sense of deprivation among VIPs and their families, which is not generally witnessed in other less ostentatious democracies. As a result, most political leaders and parties are willing to trade party loyalty or ideology to remain in office.

There is no doubt that people with integrity and honesty still exist in Indian politics, and they have proudly worked very hard to ensure the welfare and general well-being of the public. In some exceptional cases, political leaders have also given up their power, again keeping the public's well-being in mind. While it is true that many democracies such as those of Europe and the US present similar power play such as that of India, the difference has been the extent of power—mostly economic—and the government's direct and indirect domination over commercial activity. Therefore, while democracy is its own reward, and is precious to all citizens, there are costs attached to unbridled exercise of power at the political level.

10

POLITICS AND ECONOMICS

Over the years, there has been considerable introspection, debate and discussion among constitutional experts, political leaders as well as the judicial elite about legal and other changes that are necessary to make India's democracy work better for its people. The report of the National Commission to review the working of the Constitution (NCRWC), which was submitted in March 2002, had suggested various recommendations to advance the ideals, values and goals of India's democratic system. These recommendations covered a wide range of political, economic, social and legal issues, including Union–state relations and the working of Parliament and state legislatures. Here, I suggest only a few 'core' changes that are practical and can help bridge the gap between economics and politics, so that India can realize its full economic potential for the benefit of all its people.

There are a couple of proposed changes in India's parliamentary form of government, which have often figured in the public debate but which need *not* be pursued. The first is the proposal to convert India's parliamentary form of government into a presidential one. Some experts have suggested that the US-style presidential form of government is more stable and would ensure continuity of the executive branch over the specified period. The presidential form of government would also provide one known centre of executive power and enable the chief executive to form a cabinet consisting of qualified professionals from outside rather than rely exclusively on elected members of Parliament. As a result, it has been suggested that the executive branch is likely to be more competent, secure and confident in responding to the external and domestic challenges facing the nation. All this is certainly true in theory. However, the experience with the presidential form of government in several African and Latin American countries has left a great deal to be desired. Many of these countries have found themselves in deep and persistent economic crises because of the lack of checks and balances within the executive branch. In several cases, security of tenure had the perverse effect of making the chief executive non-responsive to emerging problems or unaccountable to the electorate for executive actions.

Even in a mature democracy like the US, with over two centuries of experience of the presidential form of government, the controversy over the decisions taken by the US government in several cases, illustrates the dangers inherent in vesting excessive executive authority in one person, however popular. In a developing country like India, with substantial economic power in the hands of the State, a presidential form of government could be more prone to creating a crisis of confidence. When circumstances are favourable and the economy is doing well, a single and progressive centre of executive authority can be an advantage in accelerating growth and initiating policies that may not be politically popular. However, during periods when the economy is facing an unexpected challenge or a crisis (for example, in the aftermath of the Asian economic crisis of 1997), a single centre of executive authority may not be as effective. Similarly, it is likely that in the presidential form of government, the chief executive would be less sensitive to the need for a change in the policies initiated by him/her even if the actual results turn out to be negative.

On balance, taking into account both the advantages and the disadvantages of alternative forms of government, as they have operated in other countries, the parliamentary form of government seems vastly preferable in a diverse and multifaceted polity like India's. An important advantage of the present system is simply that it has been in place since the country became independent. Despite all its shortcomings, slow deliberative processes and ups and downs (including an Emergency), the system has proved to be resilient. Established conventions, judicial pronouncements and legislative practice, based on consensus, are also vital ingredients for the functioning of a democracy in a multiparty federal republic. India now has well-established parliamentary traditions and conventions, and the main priority should be to improve its working rather than changing the system itself.

Another suggestion that has often been made, to reduce political instability, is that of elections by 'proportional representation'. Currently, a candidate to Parliament or the state legislature can be declared elected if he has the highest number of votes, even if the votes polled by him fall well short of 50 per cent of the total votes cast. This happens because of the division of the remaining votes among a number of candidates. This is also true in the case of a political party which may command a majority in Parliament even with a minority of the total votes cast in an election. In order to improve representation and to better reflect the will of the people, it has been suggested that the number of seats that a party secures in an election in a particular state should be contingent on the percentage of votes secured by it in that state or constituency. There are several variants of the proportional representation system, including a transferable voting procedure, whereby the second preference of a voter will also count if no candidate has a clear majority. In another variant, a minimum percentage of votes can be prescribed as a threshold for a party to get representation in Parliament or a legislature.

The proportional representation system certainly has the advantage of reflecting the will of the people better than the system of simple majority verdicts, or what is referred to as the first-past-the-post system. However, the proposed alternative is unduly complicated. It is also likely to be non-transparent for a large number of voters, more so when the levels of literacy and education among voters are very low. In practice, it may not reduce political instability if there are large number of parties contesting the elections and local issues, rather than national issues, dominate voter preferences. Taking these aspects into account, on balance, in India it is better to continue with the established and known system of elections by a simple majority rather than experiment with a new system, which may not yield the benefits of stability and continuity that are envisaged. For elections to yield better and more reliable electoral verdicts, which truly represent the preferred interests of the ordinary public, the best course of action is to further improve literacy and awareness among the voters.

The Economic Role of the State

The main political problem in the making of economic policy in India is not the weakness of its political institutions or its form of government, but the wrong assumptions about the real political interests at the ground level. During several decades of central planning after Independence, the primary assumption of planners, economists and development advisers was that of a welfare-maximizing State, strenuously seeking to reconcile differences among the competing demands by various groups, and selflessly promoting the greatest good of the greatest number. Based on this assumption, it was assumed that the greater the intervention of the State (and its agent, the government of the day) in the economy, the greater would be the benefit to the people. Thus, it was assumed that if the government-owned banks allocated credit, prescribed the pattern of output by giving out industrial licences and determined the pattern of consumption, the scarce economic resources of the country could be used to produce goods and services at affordable prices for the common man.

Similarly, it was assumed that if the means of production were owned by the state and were under the control of its political leaders, the entire value added in production would flow to the people. Savings and investments would also be maximized, leading to the emergence of a virtuous circle of a large public sector, leading to higher public investment, which, in turn, would lead to higher growth with distributive justice. The political motivations in the use of resources were, however, vastly different, inward looking, narrow and self-centred. Instead of a virtuous circle, the expansion of economic power by self-centred agencies of the state, over time, trapped India in a vicious circle of low growth, higher poverty and periodic economic crises.

A priority for the future is to further reduce the political role of the government in the economy. The process of reform, initiated in the early 1980s and accelerated haltingly since then, needs to be firmly pursued. The political role of the government, in so far as the economy is concerned, should be to ensure a stable and competitive environment with a strong external sector and a transparent domestic financial system. Since the balance-of-payments position, unlike in the past, is now strong, India must also adopt an aggressive open economy policy with as low a level of protection as most competitive economies in the world. Open competition is the most effective deterrent to the emergence of monopolistic practices and monopoly rents. A reduction in the political role of the government and its ministers would lead to a reduction in the ownership of commercial enterprises. The high-sounding term 'public sector' is really a misnomer in this context. The public sector does not really work for the public at large. The value added by the enterprises has been low, and instead of adding to public savings, they are now a major drain on the fiscal resources available to the government.

At the same time, the political role of the government in ensuring the availability of public goods (such as roads or water) and essential services (such as healthcare and education) must expand substantially. A reduction in the role of the government in managing commercial enterprises and an expansion of its role in the supply of public services are two sides of the same coin. A reduction in public-sector deficit and elimination of ministerial access to commercial activities will facilitate larger fiscal expenditure on public services and promote stronger ministerial responsibility for the implementation of anti-poverty and people-oriented programmes.

A related political imperative is the need for a joint agreement between leaders of major political parties and the trade unions of government employees to improve the services of the state to its people. Such an agreement to improve service to the people should be possible through a democratic process. Unfortunately, this has not been attempted and trade unions continue to press for more benefits for those who are already employed without a corresponding improvement in their duties to the public. Some public-spirited heads of municipal and state-level government departments have made attempts to meet some of the most basic requirements of the people (such as the issuance of birth certificates or the renewal of trade licences) without delay or corruption. However, even these efforts have not yielded results because of the non-cooperation of government employees. A political campaign, with the support of civil society organizations, is now necessary to make the unions and government leaders more responsive to the needs of their voters and to make public servants more accountable.

There is also a case for reducing the number of ministries and ministers in the government. Some state governments have nearly a hundred ministers, and the central government has 77 ministers (the number would have been larger if some of the parties that are supporting the present government from outside were also inside). Naturally, the larger the number of ministries and ministers, the greater is the scope for interference, conflicts and duplication. A legislative amendment to restrict the size of ministries to 15 per cent of the members of the legislatures is welcome. But even this percentage is too high. However, since the amendment has been adopted with considerable opposition from some states, it is unlikely that the number of ministries and ministers can be reduced further any time soon. An alternative approach may be to keep the numbers of ministries as they are, but redefine their functions and responsibilities.

A worthwhile principle to follow in streamlining the working of ministries may be to abolish all commercial and regulatory functions which are handled by other autonomous bodies (such as the RBI, the Securities and Exchange Board, the Telecom Commission, Electricity Commissions, the Public Sector Enterprises Board and so on). In their place, ministries should assume the responsibility of monitoring the progress of programme implementation in physical quantitative terms in areas that are of interest to the public and where there is a need for the government to assume greater responsibility.

The 'rule-making' powers of the government under the Acts of Parliament, and the complexity of various legislative provisions and rules notified by the government also require a review. Many of the Acts, including Acts for the regulation of financial or economic contracts and the development of capital markets, are more than a hundred years old. These laws are archaic and out of sync with the current realities of global trade, commerce and industry. What has made the situation worse is a plethora of rules notified by the government over several decades, many of which are not even accessible (but nevertheless remain in force). Cleaning up the legislative mess, abolishing outdated laws and simplifying the notified rules, particularly in the economic and financial areas, are essential.

Over time, the 'rule-making' powers of the government without any effective parliamentary oversight have grown immensely. The main legislative sections of an Act may be precisely defined or formulated to indicate the purpose and coverage of various provisions. However, it has become the general practice to add an explanatory section or an omnibus clause which gives powers to the government to notify various rules to give effect to legislative provisions. These rule-making powers are very wide. The legislation often prescribes that the government has the power to prescribe rules 'notwithstanding any other provisions of the Act or any other laws in force'. These omnibus powers provide sufficient scope for the arbitrary exercise of powers (or vendettas against political opponents and particular classes of persons, including taxpayers). In some states, as political rivalries among parties have intensified, these rule-making powers have been used to defeat the original purpose of the Act itself.

Small Political Parties and Their Role

Another vital political imperative for the future is to reduce the role of small political parties (with a small number of members in Parliament or legislatures) and their influence in determining a government's economic agenda. Some of these parties, with less than 5 per cent of the national votes and an even smaller number of members in Parliament, can command a disproportionate influence in the government at the Centre and pursue their own sectarian agenda.

This is a dismal state of affairs, and if small party formations, which are unrepresentative of the national will, continue to enjoy their growing clout, the economic future of the country will certainly be in jeopardy. Each party in government, however small its numbers, has become a power unto itself without being responsible to the cabinet as a whole. This is completely contrary to what was envisaged in the Constitution, and deserves to be set right as early as possible.

In most states, while a large number of parties contest elections, the government is generally formed by one party with a clear majority. Occasionally, there may also be a coalition government of two parties but, by and large, the government consists of members belonging to a single party. At the Centre, however, the trend has been in the opposite direction in the past (before 2014). For the first 42 years after Independence, up to 1989, with the exception of a three-year period, 1977–79, the Congress was voted to power with varying majority and it formed the government. After 1989, the picture changed dramatically and governments were formed by parties which did not have a clear majority by themselves. The majority support was provided by a number of pre-poll alliance parties (as in the case of the National Democratic Alliance [NDA] government from 1998 to 2004), or by post-alliance partners and supporters. During this period, there were as many as four governments that were formed by a combination of parties with a relatively small representation in Parliament with the outside support of a major party. In one case, the party that formed the government had less than even 10 per cent of the representation in the Lok Sabha. The fate of these governments naturally depended on the continued support of one or more parties outside the government, and these governments had very little room for manoeuvre when deciding policies or giving direction to the economy.

The formation of governments by parties with a relatively small presence in Parliament or by parties with the inside and outside support of a number of small parties has been an important cause of political instability during the post-1989 period (up to 2014) and its adverse consequences for governance and administration. In view of the unsatisfactory experience of the functioning of unstable and short-term governments, it is essential to make necessary legislative amendments to ensure that: (i) a government cannot be formed by a party and its pre-poll allies with, say, less than 40 per cent of the seats in Parliament with post-electoral inside or outside support of other parties; (ii) a majority government cannot be permitted to take office with outside support of a major party which has a larger number of members in the Lok Sabha than the party forming the government; and (iii) no party which has less than 10 per cent of the members in the Lok Sabha (or, say, 50 members in a House of 543 members) can be a part of the government unless it drops its separate identity as a party at the Centre and joins the leading party as an associate or an affiliate member until the next elections. In other words, very small parties which decide to be represented in the central cabinet should not have a separate identity in Parliament. Alternatively, if these small parties wish to maintain their separate identities, they can always choose to support the government from outside.

In the future, these proposals should help in reducing political instability and providing governments with greater authority to take appropriate executive decisions, particularly during periods of external or domestic economic crises or problems such as inflation or financial instability. If there is no clear or at least substantial electoral verdict in favour of a party to form a government, it would be much better to have fresh elections under a caretaker government rather than allow a new government to take office which has no clear mandate and which is not expected to last. Several of the past economic crises arose because of the inability of governments, dependent on the outside support of major parties, to take timely corrective decisions.

This was true in 1979 and again in 1990. Thus, as is well known, in 1979, India was badly affected by the oil crisis when the Janata Dal government elected in 1977 after the Emergency, was in power. However, in July 1979, in view of internal dissentions, Prime Minister Morarji Desai had to resign and Charan Singh was sworn in as the head of government with the support of the Congress from outside. This government also had to give up office after a few months because of the withdrawal of Congress support. As a result of political instability, the economic crisis became deeper and more difficult to resolve. The same situation occurred again in mid-1990, after the Gulf war, when the future of the Janata Dal government, led by V.P. Singh, became highly uncertain. The party had to split in November 1990, and a new minority government, led by Chandra Shekhar, was formed—once again with the support of the Congress from outside. The new government was, however, not allowed to present the regular budget in February 1991, and India had to go through one of the worst economic crises in its post-Independence era.

On the other hand, an important reason why economic crises were effectively tackled in 1980, and later in 1991, was the emergence of more stable governments which lasted their full term of five years. The same was true in 1997, when India was adversely affected by the aftermath of the Asian crisis. The instability in its external sector was effectively tackled by taking strong corrective measures, which at the time were unpopular and considered unconventional. After the Asian crisis, India emerged as a country with one of the strongest balance of payments in the developing world, and the country's external policies were regarded as having been highly successful and innovative. This would not have been possible if the post-1997 political outlook was unstable. Economic policy decisions to combat an emerging problem or a crisis are always politically unpopular to begin with, as they affect one or more of the special interests or activities that benefit from the existing situation. In such situations, a stable government is a necessary, though by no means sufficient, condition that makes it possible to take difficult decisions.

Elections to the Council of States

A reference was made to the growing trend of the concentration of powers in the hands of a small number of leaders and lack of inner-party democracy among political parties, large and small. This trend is nowhere more evident than in the process of elections to the Rajya Sabha, the Council of States or the so-called Upper House of Parliament. A specific number of candidates are nominated by party leaders depending on the number of seats a party has in the state assembly. Members of the legislature who are supposed to elect members to the Rajya Sabha have no choice but to vote for the candidates nominated by their parties. A candidate may have charge sheets against him for the most heinous of crimes against women or particular sections of society, or may be a financial agent of a particular party, but the legislators are forced to elect him/her to Parliament. This has caused immense damage to the reputation of an august house of Parliament in the public mind. It has also encouraged sycophancy and reduced the quality of deliberations. Taking into account the interest of the leaders of all parties in maintaining and enhancing their own powers, a radical approach to improving the process of election to the Rajya Sabha (such as direct elections on the lines of the Senate of the US) is not feasible. However, a few relatively simple changes can be made to improve the electoral process. These are:

i. A person who has been 'chargesheeted' by an agency of the central government (but not yet convicted) should not be allowed to be sworn in as a member of the Rajya Sabha. (This provision may also be made in respect of the Lok Sabha, but here political resistance may be intense). If a party still insists on electing him/her, the swearing in of such a person to the House should await the final decision of the courts. As in other important cases, courts may be requested to decide the pending case on an urgent and priority basis.

ii. Each party should nominate twice the number of candidates (or more) for every seat in the Rajya Sabha to which it is otherwise entitled. This will at least provide legislators with some choice of candidates of their own parties during elections.

iii. Elections to the Rajya Sabha should be by secret ballot so that legislators can freely exercise their votes.

iv. The domicile requirement for election to the Rajya Sabha should be restored. Since the Rajya Sabha is supposed to function as the Council of States, legislators should know the persons they are electing and candidates should have first-hand knowledge of the problems of the state. The domicile requirement should not be viewed as a narrow technical or legal requirement, but as a political requirement for effective representation of a state in the Council of States.

These changes will improve the image and working of an important political institution without substantially diminishing the present powers of parties and their leaders. It is to be hoped that these changes will command the broad support of all parties and can be implemented in the national interest without too much delay.

The Reform of Parliament Procedure

As is well known, the quality of deliberations in India's parliament is diminishing, disruptions have become common and its proceedings have become largely perfunctory. The functioning of Parliament, the maintenance of order and adherence to the rules of procedures are supposed to be under the effective control of the speaker of the Lok Sabha or the chairman of the Rajya Sabha. In actual practice, this is no longer the position. A few party leaders effectively determine whether the proceedings will continue as planned or whether these would be disrupted and the Houses adjourned for the day or even for the whole session. Individual members, other than a handful of leaders, have practically no role except to abide by the dictates of their leaders (otherwise they face the prospect of being expelled or of losing their party nominations at the next elections). There are some independent members (elected with the support of various parties) and presidential nominees in the Rajya Sabha, who are free to lodge their protests, but they are too few in number to make any difference to the final outcome.

The shrinking role of Parliament was eloquently demonstrated on 26 August 2004, when contrary to convention and well-established rules of procedure, Parliament decided to suspend the question hour, and pass the regular budget and the Finance Bill without any discussion or adequate cause (such as forthcoming elections) within a few minutes. This was the result of a back-room agreement between the leaders of parties in the government and the Opposition, following several days of disruption of parliamentary work because of a dispute on a sensitive, but extraneous, matter. The speaker or the chairman had no alternative but to go along with the agreement among the leaders of the major parties. Following the passage of the budget by a voice vote, Parliament was prorogued one week in advance of the scheduled date.

The events of 26 August constitute a new low in the working of Parliament and its democratic institutions. The passage of the Finance Bill by the representatives of the people and the Council of States without discussion was contrary to the spirit and design of the Constitution and well-established democratic conventions. It is necessary to take immediate legislative measures to avoid a recurrence of similar situations. Unfortunately, even all-party agreements on a 'Code of Conduct' or 'Rules of Procedure' are no longer sufficient to check unruly behaviour by members or the breach of agreed procedures. In case of unruly behaviour or disruption of proceedings, it is now normal for the House to be adjourned successively for a few hours at a time until the end of the day. As for breach of procedures, as long as major parties agree behind the scenes to the proposed deviation, well-established procedures can also be formally dispensed with by a voice vote inside the House. In light of the developments in parliamentary practice, suitable deterrent provisions should now be introduced by legislation (and, if necessary, by amending the Constitution) to prevent disruption of parliamentary work and suspension of rules of procedure for conduct of business.

In theory, the speaker and chairman have the powers

to expel a member from the House or suspend him/her. However, these powers have seldom been exercised. A convention has developed whereby the House can be adjourned in the event of disruption by shouting by a few members. It may be specifically provided, by legislation, that either House of Parliament cannot be adjourned more than twice in a week unless the listed business, including carried over business from previous sessions has been completed. If the members disrupt work during more than two occasions in a week, it should be incumbent on the speaker/chairman to continue with the session rather than adjourn it.

In order to help them in the conduct of parliamentary business, the leaders of the two Houses and the leaders of the Opposition may be required to nominate two persons as 'whips' from their respective parties who would be given the responsibility of ensuring that their members do not continue to disrupt the House beyond prescribed limits. If the whips are unable to exercise the necessary control over their members, they should have the authority to recommend expulsion of the unruly members from their parties. The party leaders should be expected to act on the recommendations of their whip. Alternatively, in case no penal action is taken by the parties concerned in respect of unruly members, it should be mandatory for the speaker/chairman to expel the persons nominated as whips from the House and request the leaders to appoint new persons in their place.

In case disruption of the House or breach of procedures is caused by members belonging to small parties (which are not parts of the government or the main party in the Opposition), the speaker/chairman should be required to suspend or expel the unruly members after issuing a due warning. This provision should also be codified rather than left to the discretion of the speaker/chairman. Unless the penal provisions are mandatory, it is difficult to take penal action against members of Parliament or legislators in view of the traditions of personal courtesy and apparent friendship among persons in public life in India.

Further, a legislative provision may be made to the effect that the established rules of procedure for conduct of business of the House cannot be suspended or amended after a session of Parliament has been formally convened, except in a national emergency declared by the government with the approval of the president. In other words, ad hoc and sudden suspension of rules of business, as was done on 26 August to pass the budget, must be eschewed except in an Emergency. From time to time, there may be a good case for amending the rules of procedure or business to make them more efficient. However, this should be done after due deliberation rather than all of a sudden, without adequate notice to members.

An important initiative was taken to improve the functioning of Parliament. A number of Departmental Standing Committees were set up to consider in depth the demands for grants by the ministries, and make appropriate recommendations to both Houses of Parliament before passage of the Finance Bill. Many of these all-party committees have done excellent work over the years and have made valuable suggestions. However, very little action has actually been taken by the government to implement their recommendations even though most of these have been accepted 'in principle' or 'noted' for further consideration.

To ensure a more effective follow-up, it is desirable to hold the ministry (through its secretary) accountable for implementation of recommendations accepted by the ministry. This is along the lines of the procedure adopted by the judiciary for ensuring adherence to its decisions by the ministries of the government. If the new minister wishes to change the earlier decisions of the government, he/she should be required to get the approval of Parliament after the cabinet's approval. The implementation of recommendations made by an all-party standing committee and accepted by the government should not depend on the predilections of individual ministers who happen to be in charge of a ministry.

Such changes in parliamentary procedures should enable the two Houses of Parliament to discharge the functions assigned to them by the Constitution more effectively. The proposed amendments may, however, attract opposition by some party leaders as well as political commentators on the ground that they are designed to curb the discretion and powers of members of the country's 'sovereign' Parliament and the highest legislative authority. However, the so-called 'sovereignty' of Parliament is largely a myth in the day-to-day functioning of the two Houses. All the powers available to Parliament under the Constitution are, in effect, exercised by the few leaders of parties in government and outside. The actual role of members of Parliament in determining the direction of policies, and holding the government accountable for its performance, has shrunk considerably. It is better to recognize the reality as it exists, and take necessary measures to improve the situation on the ground, rather than continue with a grand illusion about the sovereignty of Parliament and the untouchability of its procedures.

These are a few urgent issues on which action at the political level also needs to be initiated without delay. There are many other areas identified by the National Commission (2002) to improve the working of the Constitution. The implementation of the commission's recommendations by the Centre and states, after due consideration, will no doubt take a very long time. If experience is any guide, it is also not unlikely that, in view of the political differences among various parties, the report of the commission will only receive casual attention and will be shelved after some time.

Even the few suggestions made here are likely to meet with political resistance from certain quarters. However, this is a minimum agenda that the government and Parliament should consider and adopt, thus strengthening India's democratic politics.

INDEX